The

Year

of the

Poet VI

May 2019

The Poetry Posse

inner child press, ltd.

The Poetry Posse 2019

Gail Weston Shazor

Shareef Abdur Rasheed

Teresa E. Gallion

hülya n. yılmaz

Kimberly Burnham

Tzemin Ition Tsai

Elizabeth Esguerra Castillo

Jackie Davis Allen

Joe Paire

Caroline 'Ceri' Nazareno

Ashok K. Bhargava

Alicja Maria Kuberska

Swapna Behera

Albert 'Infinite' Carrasco

Eliza Segiet

William S. Peters, Sr.

General Information

The Year of the Poet VI
May 2019 Edition

The Poetry Posse

1st Edition : 2019

Publisher Information
1st Edition : Inner Child Press
intouch@innerchildpress.com
www.innerchildpress.com

$ 12.99

WHAT WOULD LIFE BE WITHOUT A LITTLE POETRY?

$\mathcal{D}$edication

This Book is dedicated to

Poetry . . .

The Poetry Posse

past, present & future

our Patrons and Readers

the Spirit of our Everlasting Muse

&

the Power of the Pen

to effectuate change!

In the darkness of my life
I heard the music
I danced . . .
and the Light appeared
and I dance

Janet P. Caldwell

Table of Contents

The Poetry Posse

Table of Contents . . . *continued*

May Featured Poets   117

Inner Child News   149

Other Anthological Works   171

$\mathcal{F}$oreword

Asia, Southeast Asia and Maritime Asia

Patchworks And Crossroads Of Arts, Culture And Tradition : Asian Perspective

Southeast Asia includes Philippines, Malaysia, Indonesia, Brunei, Laos, Cambodia, East Timor, Myanmar (Burma).

As studies reflect, Asia has always been the home to some of the biggest and the oldest civilizations. Britannica recorded ''Civilization spread from mainland Southeast Asia to China and India. Southeast Asians do not have a strong tradition of art theory or literary or dramatic criticism, for they are always more concerned with doing the actual work of producing beautiful things.'' Additionally, because the Southeast Asians, especially in the western half of the mainland, worked on nondurable materials, it is not possible to trace the development and evolution of art forms stage by stage.

According to Matt Rosenberg, a professional geographer, Asia is the largest continent in terms of size and population; Area of 17,139,445 Square Miles (44,391,162 Square Km), having

4,436,224,000 of the world's population of 7.6 billion (2017 UN estimate).

Dominating religions in Asia are Christianity, Protestantism, Islam, Hinduism, Buddhism and Shintoism and Judaism.

Asian music, dance, and songs were originally associated with tribal rituals.

Patchworks of Arts, Culture, Religion and Tradition

I have been born and brought up in The Pearl of the Orient Seas, the Philippines. I was raised at the melting pot of culture, religion and diverse ethnicity.

Philippines : Filipinos are lovers of art. Our ancestors passed their time singing corridos, and reading stories about the bravery of legendary heroes; stage dramas performed are Zarzuela and the moro-moro, forms of art which depicted the life of the people. The Philippines is a birthplace of architecture of the 16th to the 19th century which are the Baroque style churches with curved arches, altars and images of saints built by the Spaniards with the help of the Filipinos. Philippines is also dubbed as "The Fiesta Islands" because various festivals are celebrated honoring the saints, harvest and the place, are vibrant and energetic; most of them are of Hispanic influence.

Malaysia : The Malaysian society is a blend of a Malay culture, a Chinese culture, an Indian culture, a Eurasian culture, along with the cultures of the indigenous groups of the peninsula and north Borneo. Malaysians are adept at learning languages, and knowing multiple languages is commonplace. Their food has exquisite flavour, twist of Malay, Chinese, and Indian cooking. Batik-inspired designs are often produced in factories on shirts, sarongs, table cloths, or dresses forming an iconic Malaysian aesthetic. The pre-colonial Malay rulers supported a rich variety of literary figures who produced court chronicles, fables, and legends that form a prominent part of the contemporary Malaysian cultural imagination.

Indonesia : Indonesian crafts and arts are diverse: from jewelry, beadwork, batik, pottery, metal, baskets, wood carving, leather puppet, stone carving, and painting. The arts—especially painting, wood carving, dance, traditional music and puppetry—are very much alive in Indonesia. Indonesian art and culture are intertwined with religion and old traditions from the time of early migrants with Western thoughts brought by Portuguese traders and Dutch colonists. The techniques, symbolism, culture surrounding hand-dyed cotton and silk garments known as

Indonesian *Batik* permeate the lives of Indonesians from beginning to end.

Brunei : Brunei promotes the development of literature and folklore and publishes textbooks in Malay and English for use in primary and secondary schools. A form of poetry known as *sajak* is popular with schoolchildren. A number of local authors have become well known. The most famous work of traditional literature is the epic poem *Sya'ir Awang Simawn*, which recounts the exploits of the culture hero.

Laos : The rich oral tradition of poetry and folk tales possessed by the Lao-speaking people predates their written literature and maintains a wide popularity to the present day. The earliest evidence of written literature among the Lao dates from the 16th century, during the Lan Xang period. Literature served an important role as a vehicle with which to convey Buddhist religious teachings and explain proper behaviour for individuals in society. *(The Britannica)*

Cambodia : By the fourteenth century, Khmer had replaced Sanskrit as the official language. Classical Khmer represents the metaphysical union between Indian Brahmin and native Khmer of Cambodia's creation myths. It combines the multisyllabic vocabulary of Pali and Sanskrit with the largely monosyllabic, highly alliterative and onomatopoeic native vocabulary. Classical Khmer poetry has about fifty forms, using complex meters and intricate rhyme schemes. The epics, composed in thousands of stanzas, could take days to chant. *(The Britannica)*

Timor Leste : Timorese are fiercely proud of their independence and very aware of how hard they've had to fight for it. They are also quite stoic in the face of adversity, something honed through decades of tragedy. Bits of rock country, hip-flop, rap and even reggae can all be heard in East Timor's modern music. Guitars are popular and if there were garages there would be a lot of garage bands, especially in Dili. *(The Britannica)*

Myanmar : Weaving is thee Burmese's highly developed traditional art form. They have focused on writing for theater performances called *pwe* and producing texts relating to Buddhism. In addition, since the nineteenth century there is a fair amount of popular fiction. Some British fictions from the colonial period was set in Burma. The graphic arts temple sculpture in wood, stucco; temple mural painting, usually in tempera; other forms of wood and ivory carving; work in bronze, iron, and other metals; jewelry, ceramics, glassware, lacquerware, textiles and costumes.

Asian people set the paradigm of restoration, resilience and self-transcendence, not only on their beliefs but also to the way they live. Asian Contemporary writers signify long term trends and circumspection in the 21st Century literature and the global future.

Therefore, Asia is a home of cultural patchworks, heterogeneity of languages and crossroads of identity.

Caroline N. Gabis
aka. Ceri Naz

References

https://www.wordswithoutborders.org/article/cambodia-from-angkor-to-year-zero
https://amti.csis.org/defining-maritime-asia/
https://www.britannica.com/art/Southeast-Asian-arts/Indigenous-traditions
https://www.worldatlas.com/articles/the-major-religions-of-asia.html
https://www.thoughtco.com/continents-ranked-by-size-and-population-4163436

Preface

Dear Family and Friends,

Yes I am excited? This year we have aligned our vision with that of UNESCO as it honors and acknowledges a variety of Global Indigenous cultures. We are now in our sixth year of publication. As are on our way to hitting another milestone. Needless to say, I am elated. Our initial vision was to just perform at this level for the year of 2014. Since that time we have had the blessed opportunity to include many other wonderful word artists and storytellers in the Poetry Posse from lands, cultures and persuasions all over the world. We have featured hundreds of additional poets, thereby introducing their poetic offerings to our vast global readership.

In keeping with our effort and vision to expand the awareness of poets from all walks by making this offerings accessible, we at Inner Child Press International will continue to make every volume a FREE Download. The books are also available for purchase at the affordable cost of $7.00 per volume.

In the previous years, our monthly themes were Flowers, Birds, Gemstones, Trees and Past

Cultures. This year we have elected to continue the Cultural theme. In each month's volume you will have the opportunity to not only read at least one poem themed by our Poetry Posse members about such culture, but we have included a few words about the culture in our prologue. The reasoning behind this is that now our poetry has the opportunity to be educational for not only the reader, but we poets as well. We hope you find the poetic offerings insightful as we use our poetic form to relay to you what we too have learned through our research in making our offering available to you, our readership.

In closing, we would like to thank you for being an integral part of our amazing journey.

Enjoy our amazing featured poets . . . they are amazing!

Building Cultural Bridges of Understanding . . .

Bless Up . . . From the home in our hearts to yours

Bill

The Poetry Posse
Inner Child Press Ineternational

PS

Do Not forget about the World Healing, World Peace Poetry effort.

Available here

<u>www.worldhealingworldpeacepoetry.com</u>

**For Free Downloads of Previous Issues of
The Year of the Poet**

<u>www.innerchildpress.com/the-year-of-the-poet</u>

poetry is . . . .

Asia, Southeast Asia and Maritime Asia

Geographically, Asia, Southeast Asia and Maritime Asia represents a diverse beauty that exemp[lifies a mostly tropical type of setting with access to many seas and oceans. The collection of cultures to be found inhabiting these lands are equally diverse in their living, social intergartion and spiritual expressions. From Viet Nam to the Philippines to Cambodia and Malaysia and all other countries in this region there can be found a myriad of languages and dialects. The lifestyles also vary in many different ways.

For more information visit

https://en.wikipedia.org/wiki/Maritime_Southeast_Asia

Poets . . .
sowing seeds in the
Conscious Garden of Life,
that those who have yet to come
may enjoy the Flowers.

Poets, Writers . . . know that we are the enchanting magicians that nourishes the seeds of dreams and thoughts . . . it is our words that entice the hearts and minds of others to believe there is something grand about the possibilities that life has to offer and our words tease it forth into action . . . for you are the Poet, the Writer to whom the Gift of Words has been entrusted . . .

~ wsp

I FLY

because

...said the Dreamer to the world.

I Can

www.iamjustbill.com

The Year of the Poet VI

May 2019

The Poetry Posse

Poetry succeeds where instruction fails.

~ wsp

Gail Weston Shazor

Gail Weston Shazor

This is a creative promise ~ my pen will speak to and for the world. Enamored with letters and respectful of their power, I have been writing for most of my life. A mother, daughter, sister and grandmother I give what I have been given, greatfilledly.

Author of . . .

"An Overstanding of an Imperfect Love"
&
Notes from the Blue Roof

Lies My Grandfathers Told Me

available at Inner Child Press.

www.facebook.com/gailwestonshazor
www.innerchildpress.com/gail-weston-shazor
navypoet1@gmail.com

Sijo

When counting my blessings, I always think of you

For you are my moon and stars, my waking and rest

I breathe the mist from your flowing waters

On This Beach

They arrived on this beach
On this beach shoeless
The tears done and grim
For that had already been shed
On the journey
And in it's place
A stoic waiting on the next

They gripped the rags and tatters
Rags and tatters that make
Them all look the same
Dark skinned
And dirt skinned
And none knowing the where
That they are

And the new ones are restless
Ones are restless
Born in between then and now
There is no belonging
To anywhere
No official passport
Or certificates to name them

Numbered up quickly against waves
Quickly against waves
And no one will stop to count grains
Drops spilled in water
And the predators
Have left their shallowness
For places in sand

And the drums continued to beat
Continued to beat the count
So that they knew just how many
Were thrown over
The hulls of whitewashed
Soulless hulls bobbing
In the surf

When I find myself on the edge
On the edge of the water
I can hear their cries
Because the matter of the world
Has not changed
The sand remains
The same grain

As countless as the stars in the sky
The stars in the sky shine
And as you lift up your eyes
Remember
That that happened
Under your feet and you stand
On holy ground

liming

Green leaves greening
Water falls watering
Call bird calling
Yellow sun yellowing
Nappy hair napping
Bud trees budding
House old housing
Grey concrete greying
Parrot plumes parroting
Plant gardener planting
Tingle bells tingling
Risen people rising
Love you loving

Gail Weston Shazor

Alicja Maria Kuberska

.

Alicja Maria Kuberska – awarded Polish poetess, novelist, journalist, editor. She was born in 1960, in Świebodzin, Poland. She now lives in Inowrocław, Poland.

In 2011 she published her first volume of poems entitled: "The Glass Reality". Her second volume "Analysis of Feelings", was published in 2012. The third collection "Moments" was published in English in 2014, both in Poland and in the USA. In 2014, she also published the novel - "Virtual roses" and volume of poems "On the border of dream". Next year her volume entitled "Girl in the Mirror" was published in the UK and "Love me" , " (Not)my poem" in the USA. In 2015 she also edited anthology entitled "The Other Side of the Screen".

In 2016 she edited two volumes: "Taste of Love" (USA), "Thief of Dreams" (Poland) and international anthology entitled " Love is like Air" (USA). In 2017 she published volume entitled "View from the window" (Poland). She also edits series of anthologies entitled "Metaphor of Contemporary" (Poland)

Her poems have been published in numerous anthologies and magazines in Poland, the USA, the UK, Albania, Belgium, Chile, Spain, Israel, Canada, India, Italy, Uzbekistan, Czech Republic, South Korea and Australia. She was a featured poet of New Mirage Journal (USA) in the summer of 2011.

Alicja Kuberska is a member of the Polish Writers Associations in Warsaw, Poland and IWA Bogdani, Albania. She is also a member of directors' board of Soflay Literature Foundation.

Madagascar

At the end of the world is a scrap of Gondawa
- a huge island slowly drifting through time

Isolation, in the act of creation, gave a different course of evolution
and it amazed with its richness of the forms and colors of nature

In the land of lemurs with big, sad eyes,
life took on unprecedented and amazing shapes

Indian Ocean with clear as crystal waters
affectionately embraces white beaches with its blue arms

In the underwater treasury, just below the surface of the water,
it hides wonderful corals and run of colorful fish

Warm wind blows carry on tirelessly
From the heart of the land a sweet aroma of ripe vanilla pods

Border

The wide open window invites into the apartment
fresh air and the inquisitive eyes of passers-by.
A warm wind threw inside handful of petals torn from an
apple tree.
It brought in the aroma of blooming flowers in the
backyard garden..
In the empty room can be heard a joyful chirping
and the loud laughter of children playing with a colorful
ball

They call you - an autistic child

You live alone in a closed cube block,
in an always empty and quiet space.
In your world, touch hurts and sounds are audible.
A soundproof glass separates you
from the voice of another human being
You paint on it with your fingers and leave a trace.
It is your way of trying to contact.

It is difficult to escape
from the sealed trap of one's own mind.

Eros

The first gods emerged from nonexistence
Gaia covered her nakedness with the veil of greenery
Uranus dressed himself with clouds flowing across the sky
The winged Eros was given a bow and quiver with arrows

God of love released a few arrows and breathed life sparks
This beautiful young man, an inseparable companion of
Aphrodite,
possessed bitter and sweet power to hurt human hearts

When Eros smiles and releases the golden arrow
The girl unravels the braid for her lover, puts flowers in her
hair
She can, like a feather, swirl high above the cloudlets

When Eros frowns and chooses the iron arrow
unbridled lust and brutal strength is awaked in a boy's mind
The girl's hair falls to the ground, fear is born in her eyes

Mighty Eros, break your iron arrows, use only gold ones.
Let the girls wait eagerly for their beloveds
- sing songs and write poems about glorious and eternal
love

Jackie Davis Allen

Jackie Davis Allen, otherwise known as Jacqueline D. Allen or Jackie Allen, grew up in the Cumberland Mountains of Appalachia. As the next eldest daughter of a coal miner father and a stay at home mother, she was the first in her family to attend and graduate from college. Her siblings, in their own right, are accomplished, though she is the only one, to date, that has discovered the gift of writing.

Graduating from Radford University, with a Bachelors of Science degree in Early Education, she taught in both public and private schools. For over a decade she taught private art classes to children both in her home and at a local Art and Framing Shop where she also sold her original soft sculptured Victorian dolls and original christening gowns.

She resides in northern Virginia with her husband, taking much needed get-aways to their mountain home near the Blue Ridge Mountains, a place that evokes memories of days spent growing up in the Appalachian Mountains.

A lover of hats, she has worn many. Following marriage to her college sweetheart, and as wife, mother, grandmother, teacher, tutor, artist, writer, poet and crafter, she is a lover of art and antiques, surrounding herself, always, with books, seeking to learn more.

In 2015 she authored *Looking for Rainbows, Poetry, Prose and Art*, and in 2017, *Dark Side of the Moon*. Both books of mostly narrative poetry were published by Inner Child Press and were edited by hulya n. yilmaz.

http://www.innerchildpress.com/jackie-davis-allen.php
jackiedavisallen.com

News Flash: Through War's Infused Lens

Destruction.
Descending down like a plague,
fear spreads its harm all around.
The evil that is war,
is never satisfied.

With swollen heart
of wicked need and greed,
violence reigns, overtakes the land.
Litters it with putrid deposits
of mangled bodies.

Sacrificing wealth.
With small treasures, she boldly
bribes Border Guards. Day and night.
For the right to fish, to provide.
To feed her wanting children.

Petite, talented
haute couture, French speaking.
A mother exercises plot
of desperation: a deception.
With grit and determination.

Toughened, empowered,
trusting in God, she in uncouth disguise,
is now a fisherman. Daily, she places
In her boat her catch. Beneath the floorboards.
Her anesthetized children, too.

Then, one night, prepared,
sudden moment realized,
with guards lulled into habit's stupor,
she seizes opportunity.
Risks everything. No turning back.

With guns, protocol, laid aside,
inebriated, (incredulously)
and with greed's thirst, the guards
rejoice that the proffered bags,
are filled with coveted valuables.

Gold, silver, rubies,
emeralds, diamonds. Pearls?
And the mother, with palpitation,
paddles her shell shocked innocents
toward freedom's hospitable shore.

Finally, thankfully, safely ashore,
Distanced, and far from the battleground,
Refuge soothes some fears. A Vietnamese
mother prays rescue, escape, safety
for those left behind. Prays reunion, too.

I Was There

Vietnam. Too many decades, inpregnated with fear.
Bullets flying, sanity missing. Hope, too.
The stench and the sight of the dead and dying,
All too real: a nightmare's existence.

No way to explain this ungodly war.

My children are white
Like the ghosts pointing fingers at them.
All too real are the skeletons hanging in trees.
Insanity has taken up residence. Inside. Outside.

Unrelenting evil. Night and day.

The POW camps are filled, overflowing.
With dissenters. My husband. A child, too.
Are they still alive? And those hiding they are trying
To survive. In ways unspeakable.

This is Vietnam.

My once high status means nothing now, only
The staunch determination inside my head.
I am orchestrating a plan of escape.
Strengthening my body, my resolve.

I have become a fisherman.

I stow away my children
Down beneath, where I place the fish, my haul.
So that we might eat. The Border Guards,
Lulled into habit, believe I am no threat.
To their prowess, to their power.

My children lie in the fishes keep.
Drugged to keep them quiet, unaware.
Out into the jungle's dark night I go.
I am simply a fisherman. But no! I am desperate.

Resolute, unwavering, I move toward freedom.

By the slight light of the diminished moon
I steady my heart, my nerves.
Mind focused upon the subterfuge,
I row the boat toward the predetermined route.

Leaving my home, leaving all. Except . . .

In canvas bags, stained, and scented
With the remains of day's catch, is the lure.
Approaching the guards, I am now more
Friend than foe. They think.

Curious, they allow me to come close.

Inebriated with excitement, eyes agog,
They open the bags I toss at their feet,
And are blinded by their sudden wealth.
By my family's silver, gold, jewelry.

We escape through the window of their avarice.

When Does Peace Begin

Thinking back over rights
And wrongs, dwelling
On those things that rise up
As stumbling blocks,

Like past days and past ways.
Of some time long gone.
Of some gone right,
Of some gone wrong.

Conscious awakens in me,
The time which is now:
The time to grant
A right to someone

Who has been wronged.
Like my mother used to say,
Two wrongs in the doing
Do not make a right.

Yet, I can not believe it.
What he said. What he did.
How could he? My tears fell.
As did my self esteem.

The world seemed at an end.
No one cared. No one came
To comfort me. Suddenly, a voice
Silenced my pathetic cries.

Something deep within
Called out to me to join in prayer,
To rise up, to dust off
My self centered thoughts.

And to lift up in prayer
All those in harm's way.
Those, the innocent ones.
Those whose lives are threatened.

Those, whose very existence, stand
On the precipice of life and death;
While I, blessed am able
To give more

Of what I have been given:
Love, hope, prayers,
Comfort, friendship.
Companionship

In this moment
I find my heart calling me
To a higher level of grace.
Calling me to a place

Where my own wants
And needs seem small.
Little in comparison.
Childish and insignificant.

Let us be empowered by love,
Forgiving others, ourselves.
Let us try to make a difference
In the lives of those we meet.

Jackie Davis Allen

Tzemin Ition Tsai

Dr. Tzemin Ition Tsai (蔡澤民博士) was born in Republic of China, in 1957. He holds a Ph.D. in Chemical Engineering and two Masters of Science in Applied Mathematics and Chemical Engineering. He is a professor at Asia University (Taiwan), editor of "Reading, Writing and Teaching" academic text. He also writes the long-term columns for Chinese Language Monthly in Taiwan.

He is a scholar with a wide range of expertise, while maintaining a common and positive interest in science, engineering and literature member.

He has won many national literary awards. His literary works have been anthologized and published in books, journals, and newspapers in more than 40 countries and have been translated into more than a dozen languages.

Why The China Rose Tinted Top Of The Fence Red?

The fog never knew where it came from fill the valley full
Faded out indifferently a hint of coolness
A corner of the roof of that old house
Obscured and covered up
Deep in the shadows behind the thick trees
Teasing of senses but seems to be nothing
Always successfully escaped from my eyes tracking
The red-painted heavy door has been locked for hundreds
of years
The China Rose never voluntarily lonely
Probed one after another and tinted the top of the fence red
To seduce south winds
With a silent sigh
Could you have forgotten that the faster he come, the faster
he go
Knowingly
There is nothing worthwhile to talk about without the
promise of love

While the valley was falling down a vast rain unpredictably
Not hurried nor rushed
Several green ducks fall outside the fence were chasing and
biting each other
The rain dragged its feet slowly along
How could she know how many solitaries the pond has
drunk?
With that little bit of my absent-minded
Unexpectedly already can't recover the leisurely blowing
song which was getting gradually away
The red-painted heavy door still didn't move at all
That agreement with dandelions about the spring of earth

Invited full of the greenery of the mountains
Bursts of fragrance
The dances of white-jade butterflies so Maniac
How could not know
The number of the thieves who steal flowers are always
greatly more than the flower-cherisher

When I Am Chasing That Waves

The water gurgling away
Like the beauty's eye-wave that looks into the distance
The mountain is lying
Such as the beauty's eyebrows that raised up
Follow the light and the road
Ask my friend where to go?
Echo back from the distance
Did not answer me
Walked over to where the landscape intersection
Discovered that spring has not been far away
Now
Have to say goodbye to my friend
Send you a swift horse
Not to let you catch up with the spring
But want you to come back quickly
Enjoy with you
Taking advantage of these beautiful scenery

Unrelenting Spring Breeze

A spring breeze blew over
Cause the wind chimes to jingle-jangle ring
Falling maple leafs take away my care
A spring breeze blew over
Agitate the flag on the sail
Sea level whistling warm up ocean rolling

The spring breeze has no willing to change
Looking around for whales within the four seas
Unpredictable channels
Where? What shape? What mood? and How to peace of my
mind?
Forgetting to make yourself in a vague sense
Leave a hint of exclamation
When is my heart no longer hurt?

Sometimes the sun will forget our appointments
Why is dark night sure to come every day?
Follow the course of the Big Dipper
Maybe you can still find the dreamy romantic spring breeze
Under the bright moon
You can never lose
That front line of footprints

Tzemin Ition Tsai

Shareef
Abdur
Rasheed

Shareef Abdur Rasheed

Shareef Abdur-Rasheed, AKA Zakir Flo was born and raised in Brooklyn, New York. His education includes Brooklyn College, Suffolk County Community College and Makkah, Saudi Arabia. He is a Veteran of the Viet Nam era, where in 1969 he reverted to his now reverently embraced Islamic Faith. He is very active in the Islamic community and beyond with his teachings, activism and his humanity.

Shareef's spiritual expression comes through the persona of "Zakir Flo" . Zakir is Arabic for "To remind". Never silent, Shareef Abdur-Rasheed is always dropping science, love, consciousness and signs of the time in rhyme.

Shareef is the Patriarch of the Abdur-Rasheed Family with 9 Children (6 Sons and 3 Daughters) and 41 Grandchildren (24 Boys and 17 Girls).

For more information about Shareef, visit his personal FaceBook Page at :

https://www.facebook.com/shareef.abdurrasheed1
https://zakirflo.wordpress.com

Asia

amazing continent
unbelievably diverse
unbelievably vast
unbelievably rich
comprising of more then
50 countries
myriad of languages, cultures,
peoples and their tribes
and nations
the largest continent on earth
which is home to 4.5 billion
60% of mother earth's population
from Afghanistan to Yemen
it bogles the mind to digest
true embodiment of diversity
China 1.4 billion
Shanghai biggest city
India 1.3 billion
Yangtze third largest river
Everest almost 30'000 ft high
tallest point on earth
dead sea at minus 1295 ft
the lowest
Russia alone,
40% of Asia's land mass
hundreds of languages spoken
more than one billion speak mandarin
India 30 or more languages
Asia mind blowing vastness, richness,
Asia massive
contributed much to human kind
globally

science, mathematics, architecture,
literature, technology, art, music
on ' n ' on
what more can i say
to many props/tributes to pay
Asia, major factor, player, actor
as matter a fact a giant to be exact

food4thought =education

in moonlight..,

in first saw her
light cascaded
off her face
i was frozen in place
seemed so surreal
moonlight night revealed
beauty superb unique
hardly a verb can speak
we all dream of extraordinary
things magnificent
but she was more than this
exquisite, moon highlighted
features
appeared to reach a zenith
captivated senses, motivated,
generated heat so much
i was drenched in sweat
one would think i landed
on the sun
but no, it was effect of
divine nectar dispatched
through moon beams that
penetrated my heart
just then i heard a voice
penetrate the dark say
" *Fajr "
time to get up and pray
she and moonlight went away

food4thought = education

*Fajr = morning prayer between
break of dawn and sunrise

fog..,

settles in like it's comfortable
surreal feel touches me inwardly
strange scene i see
visibility disability
certainly, obviously
though enhancing spiritually
can also benefit physically
as peace emanates from thickness
soothing elixir, impromptu fixer
of new, even old wounds,
sore souls, stressful woes
can heal soon
something simple yet profoundly
calming
step back for a moment
slowly, deliberately
exit the mad pace
take a look at the face of tranquility
tuck it away in your memory
simple as it may seem
simplicity can redeem
simple as it may seem
so quiet, calming
relaxing, healing

food4thought = education

Shareef Abdur Rasheed

Kimberly Burnham

Kimberly Burnham

Find yourself in the pattern. As a 28-year-old photographer, Kimberly Burnham appreciated beauty. Then an ophthalmologist diagnosed her with a genetic eye condition saying, "Consider life, if you become blind." She discovered a healing path with insight, magnificence, and vision. Today, 33 years later, a poet and neurosciences expert with a PhD in Integrative Medicine, Kimberly's life mission is to change the global face of brain health. Using health coaching, Reiki, Matrix Energetics, craniosacral therapy, acupressure, and energy medicine, she supports people in their healing from brain, nervous system, and chronic pain issues. As managing editor of Inner Child Magazine, Kimberly's 2019 project is peace, language, and visionary poetry with her recently published book, *Awakenings: Peace Dictionary, Language and the Mind, a Daily Brain Health Program.*

http://www.NerveWhisperer.Solutions
https://www.linkedin.com/in/kimberlyburnham

The Northern Most Eight

Eight with land within an Arctic Circle
if we start with the most Russia
where peace is reflected "mir" "мир"
then clockwise Finland Sweden Norway
where peace is experienced as "ȓauha" "fred" and again
"fred"

The people of a small island of Grimsey
find Icelandic peace in "friður"
and in the Danish spoken in Greenland "fred" again
then a long Canadian arc through the Yukon, Northwest
Territories, and Nunavut
a short hop through the Alaskan United States
and back into Russia

Do we even notice everywhere
there are circumpolar peoples
a linguistic and cultural umbrella
protecting hiding covering
various indigenous peoples of the Arctic
communities who each think of peace in a different way
"irqigsiniq" in Kalaallisut or Greenlandic
"haimmahi" the West Inuktitut of Canada
"lalʸlɨ wəlupsɨ" in Khanty or Ostyak in Northern Russia
whatever the word each of us seeking peace

Rivers and Languages

There are three great Siberian rivers
flowing into the Arctic Ocean
the largest is the Yenisei
the Ket people who live along her shores
say peace "unaat" or in Cyrillic letters "унаат"

Write "унаат" in a single line
tracing the curves of the "У" jumping next to the "Н"
"А" "А" followed by "Т"
like a long river winding her way into the Arctic
languages and peoples elegantly dancing
show scientists our connections
to each other and our nature

The Ket language spoken by a small group of forest hunters
in the Yenisei River area of Russian central Siberia
are related to North America's Tlingit
Eyak and Athabaskan speaking people
we are all connected

Cedar Peace and Calm

The Siberian cedar
a stone pine "Larix decidua"
sacred tree of Tubalars
a symbol of the power
beauty and courage
an old man tree represents
a sage in fairy tales
among these northern people of Russia
who call peace by the name "tegin"
simple and peaceful
from the Altay "tegin" meaning for no reason
ordinary and just
like peace should be everywhere
freeing us to eat the cedar nuts full of protein
and calm inducing tryptophan

Elizabeth E. Castillo

Elizabeth Esguerra Castillo is a multi-awarded and an Internationally-Published Contemporary Author/Poet and a Professional Writer / Creative Writer / Feature Writer / Journalist / Travel Writer from the Philippines. She has 2 published books, "Seasons of Emotions" (UK) and "Inner Reflections of the Muse", (USA). Elizabeth is also a co-author to more than 60 international anthologies in the USA, Canada, UK, Romania, India. She is a Contributing Editor of Inner Child Magazine, USA and an Advisory Board Member of Reflection Magazine, an international literary magazine. She is a member of the American Authors Association (AAA) and PEN International.

Web links:

Facebook Fan Page

https://free.facebook.com/ElizabethEsguerraCastillo

Google Plus

https://plus.google.com/u/0/+ElizabethCastillo

The Lumads

Indigenous tribe from the south,
Of the Philippine archipelago
Armed with an exotic culture
Though a part of the minority.

Others view them having low stature
Industrious by nature, they strive,
To gain good education
And have meaningful lives.

Along the mountainous region and sacred valleys,
The eccentric Lumads dwell
Guarding their territories
Protecting their ancestral lands.

Rituals, dances, and chants,
Comprise their rich culture
Enchanting tourists from all around.

Silenced Voice

What is freedom without choice
When they keep suppressing the majority's voice?
What is freedom when you choose
To be blind, to be a mere slave
Tolerating tyranny, a silenced voice in the dark-
Liberty was not just blind-folded
The oppressed were even forced not to speak
Even if the truth should be heard
In the four corners of our Motherland.
A silenced voice with hatred echoing within this madness-
Sign of the times- the guilty are set free
While the innocent and honest are held captive-
Silenced voice, pleading, eyes bearing sadness
Soul shouting to the innermost well of an ailing humanity
Denied precious freedom, when will be the dawning of a
new day?
Raging light, fighting demons into the night,
Do not be silenced, do not give in to fright.

Alchemic Love

I've carved the words on the moon's surface
And created an alchemy,
Mortals carve their names on barks of a tree
But mine's etched on the lunar plane,
For the Universe to lay witness
Of my immortal love for you...
A love so strong, it moves the tides
An infinite love without boundaries,
A love written in the sands of time
Older than the history of Adam and Eve...

Joe
Paire

Joe Paire

Joseph L Paire' aka Joe DaVerbal Minddancer . . .
is a quiet man, born in a time where civil liberties
were a walk on thin ice. He's been a victim of his
own shyness often sidelined in his own quest for
love. He became the observer, charting life's path.
Taking note of the why, people do what they do.
His writings oft times strike a cord with the
dormant strings of the reader. His pen the rosined
bow drawn across the mind. He comes full-frontal
or in the subtlest way, always expressing in a way
that stimulate the senses.

www.facebook.com/joe.minddancer

Joe Paire

A Change Of View

You told me he was the enemy
He showed me he is a friend
How can one dictate hate
In a land where you've never been
This war is over and a new one begins

Southeast Asia Vietnam in particular
Something happened diplomacy snapped
Now I'm told how to deal with you
What in the world is this world coming to
Are we to be walled in from me and you?

So many delicacies let's share the recipes
Clothing and spices agricultural devices
Why be so divisive when the world is priceless
Let's travel a little further east
where my friend found his wife at

The Philippines of island dreams
The color schemes of a wedding
We're dressed in Emerald and cream
We're blessed by the one whom we believe in
There was dancing and drink all through the evening

I started thinking if this world would just be still
If we could really start anew
I would strive with all my heart
To change our point of view

A Night In Singapore

I'm digging the night life
I'm checking out the sights
Neon signs and clear plastic heels
I'm getting Bangkok dangerous chills
Jakarta where are you? I have a taste for your thrills
But what do I know besides movies and spill
I know someone who lived there but still
What do I know?
There are folk there who never travel
Yet I'm tasked to set the gavel of knowledge
Now granted I've traveled through Europe and beyond
But the Southeast of Asia I've yet to put foot on
China and Japan a mere fantasies
I've been to France and lived romantic dreams
20 years old on the French riviera
Edenborough Scotland and what have you
But west it seems lives in California dreams
I go west to fulfill my east
Southeast Asia you're my treat

Time Is Precious

I lost too many friends last year
Family and a couple of peers last year
I've shed no tears as of yet
So I'm trying to live in the moment blessed
Would have, could have, should have
Are nothing more than words of regret
What do we have but time But we don't have time
Plans that don't pan out are taking time from my mind
Everything isn't going to work out every day every time
So yes, time is precious or am I just restless
I calculate immortality into my reality with the casualties of
a guest list. I guess this time was wasted
not consuming what I've tasted
Maybe too much day to day has been taken mistakenly
The cost of time usually be breaking me
Bad movies, bad books but we took the time to have a look
We even make time into day time just to save time for
some playtime, some me time
Sometimes we time; Breakfast lunch and dinner
Is sleep a waste of time or stuck at home in winter
What can you do when the time is against you
The clock keeps on running
Sometimes we just skip through
multitasking is like a staple
It allows you to do more with the time you're allotted for
But we never do, Dinner at 8 you arrive at 10
2 hours wasted just figuring what to wear styling your hair
Searching for tickets you can't find anywhere
They've been in your pocket time ain't rocket science
The clock in compliance, locked in reliance
Friends or clients time is precious

hülya

n.

yılmaz

A retired Liberal Arts professor, hülya n. yılmaz [sic] is Co-Chair and Director of Editing Services at Inner Child Press International, and a literary translator. Her poetry has been published in an excess of sixty anthologies of global endeavors. Two of her poems are permanently installed in *TelePoem Booth*, a nation-wide public art exhibition in the U.S. She has shared her work in Kosovo, Canada, Jordan and Tunisia. hülya has been honored with a 2018 WIN Award of British Colombia, Canada. She is presently working on three poetry books and a short-story collection. hülya finds it vital for everyone to understand a deeper sense of self and writes creatively to attain a comprehensive awareness for and development of our humanity.

hülya n. yılmaz, Ph.D.

Writing Web Site
hulyanyilmaz.com

Editing Web Site
hulyasfreelancing.com

shipwrecks

how cold-bloodedly do we unearth our discoveries . . .

archaeology faces many a challenge on land
Earth's layers are multitudinous, after all
unlike shipwrecks – the so-called "time capsules" . . .

hence, the word of the day: just do it with ease!

let us keep on learning about our objects . . .

who cares about the persons whose lives
were wrecked in those ships?

let us keep on learning about our objects . . .

come on, look at all these ceramics!
these finds are from merely seven shipwrecks
between the 14th and the 19th centuries, mind you . . .
one exhibition resides in Kuala Lumpur, Malaysia
the museum goes by the name of "Muzium Negara"
make sure to pay that place a visit during your tour
perhaps you will return with a gift du jour

"Time capsules", states one of our modern-day sources
and adds, "the advantages of shipwreck sites" . . . to boost

let us keep on learning about our objects . . .

a HAIKU too can cry

the Sun shines brightly
meadows miss the innocent
children died again

her tears

in the still of the night,
amid complete strangers in uniform
keeping her away from her Mommy,
she is crying shriek wails
her face, trauma-distorted
in its meant-to-be beautiful glow

a mere 2-year-old child

innocence lost
purity, no more

a cold-blooded picture
speaks on her behalf

language . . .
what is it good for
when pain is inflicted
on purity, on the core love
between a mother and her baby?

losing it . . .
the tongue and all

the heart aches yet once again
and hurts on and on and on

where has compassion gone?

Teresa E. Gallion

Teresa E. Gallion was born in Shreveport, Louisiana and moved to Illinois at the age of 15. She completed her undergraduate training at the University of Illinois Chicago and received her master's degree in Psychology from Bowling Green State University in Ohio. She retired from New Mexico state government in 2012.

She moved to New Mexico in 1987. While writing sporadically for many years, in 1998 she started reading her work in the local Albuquerque poetry community. She has been a featured reader at local coffee houses, bookstores, art galleries, museums, libraries, Outpost Performance Space, the Route 66 Festival in 2001 and the State of Oklahoma's Poetry Festival in Cheyenne, Oklahoma in 2004. She occasionally hosts an open mic.

Teresa's work is published in numerous Journals and anthologies. She has two CDs: *On the Wings of the Wind* and *Poems from Chasing Light*. She has published three books: *Walking Sacred Ground, Contemplation in the High Desert* and *Chasing Light.*

Chasing Light was a finalist in the 2013 New Mexico/Arizona Book Awards.

The surreal high desert landscape and her personal spiritual journey influence the writing of this Albuquerque poet. When she is not writing, she is committed to hiking the enchanted landscapes of New Mexico. You may preview her work at

http://bit.ly/1aIVPNq or *http://bit.ly/13IMLGh*

Kingdom of Cambodia

Some of the most beautiful landscapes
on planet earth embrace Cambodia.
And they are tainted by trails of blood
from the inhumanity of humankind.

Your history of war and genocide
has a long tail dragging back
to the 15th century.

Interference from outsiders is like
a plaque on your history through the years.
It has not helped but made your survival
as a country tenuous at best.

While the poverty rate has been reduced,
government corruption puts your country
on a slippery slope that could lead to disaster.

Night Play

Evening's silent approach brings closure.
The iris closes its windows to protect
its delicate stems from night's dark work.

The sand complains in swirls
as little night creatures
face the darkness without fear.

The moon creates a shadow road
for mercenaries. Owl, fox, wolf, bats
come out for a feeding. Like humans,
they need daily renewal to grow strong.

Donkeys sleep peacefully in the barn
while the word apprentice holds
candlelight vigil with the blank page.
Strength of love moves the pen.

Midwest Frigid

I step into the frigid morning,
scan the salt and pepper snow
holding the ground hostage.
The annual seduction of a
cityscape we take for granted.

A vision of stored memories
reminds me of snowcapped
mountains in the far west
suckling ice sculptures hanging
from trees that decorate mountainsides.

Reality is the stained white blanket
of a Midwest winter seized by gray
light and subzero temperatures
greeting me at the front door.

I know that even underneath
these scales of pollution there is love,
laughter, pain, suffering and life
moving forward.

History is created with the passage
of each minute just like my vision
of serene mountains and every
other destination clinging
to the earth sphere.

Ashok K. Bhargava

Ashok K. Bhargava

Ashok Bhargava is a poet, writer, community activist, public speaker, management consultant and a keen photographer. Based in Vancouver, he has published several collections of his poems: Riding the Tide, Mirror of Dreams, A Kernel of Truth, Skipping Stones, Half Open Door and Lost in the Morning Calm. His poetry has been published in various literary magazines and anthologies.

Ashok is a Poet Laureate and poet ambassador to Japan, Korea and India. He is founder of WIN: Writers International Network Canada. Its main objective is to inspire, encourage, promote and recognize writers of diverse genres, artists and community leaders. He has received many accolades including Nehru Humanitarian Award for his leadership of Writers International Network Canada, Poets without Borders Peace Award for his journeys across the globe to celebrate peace and to create alliances with poets, and Kalidasa Award for creative writings.

A Day In Paradise

Like pearls scattered in clear water
Alamino's "Hundred Islands"
on the fins of the rainbow fish
come to a sparkling shine
at the crack of dawn.

Exotic flowers
in a procession of colors
eagerly spray fragrance
on the white sands and surfs
of the isolated beaches.

Children make
sand castles and genitals
to the amusement of people
but the mindless waves swallow them
without leaving a sign.

Women chatter over the crackling
flames of the charcoal barbeque
men gulp San Miguel down their throats
dance and sing songs
as cool breeze lull them deep into heaven.

What's the point in flying
thousands of miles away
from the Oregon coast
to salivate on guavas in salty air
Alice could not figure out.

As the sun begins to hide
behind the hills

people rush back to the city
beneath the freshly ploughed sky
enhancing beauty of the playful sea.

Soon the night starts to unfold
colors of flowers dissolve into shades of grey
as shaking heads in the dark winds
flowers begin to plan for
another day in the tropical paradise.

The Hundred Islands is a National Park in Alaminos in the Philippines / Maritime Asia.

Barrio Santa Cruz

Over the flat farms
blossoms a pink morning sun
at the hawker's call for fresh pandesal.

In the bright rays of the rising sun
violet, red, white and yellow flowers
create a carnival of colors.

Tin roofs of stilted houses
stretch like waves
and vanish into distant ocean.

Contrasted against the lush green trees
the barrio looks dyed
in a multitude of colors.

If this were a Bollywood movie
the native girls would be dancing
to the rustic tunes of handsome boys.

I want to absorb the fragrance of sampaguita
and cool shade of acacia with the hope
that it will help me dream this view into immortality.

Pandesal or pan de sal, is a common bread roll made of flour, eggs, yeast, sugar, and salt. Usually the hawkers sell freshly baked bread rolls in the morning.

Bollywood is the Indian movie industry, based in Mumbai (Bombay).

Sampaguita is a sweetly scented tropical flower belonging to the wide genus of Jasmine in Southeast Asia.

Balungao

The lady rolling a big tobacco leaf is indifferent
to the "fresh juice for sale" sign
hanging on the stump of a tree that bleeds
nectar and the glimpse of a dormant volcano
so evident from the plaza square.

A hungry child suck on
the tender breasts of her mom
as a bunch of kids hop around
on the stilts to the envy of a
water buffalo disciplined by
a demanding farmer.

Ear blasting sounds of jeepneys
and tricycles mingled with
cock's roost, dog's bark and blurting radios
can't disturb the eternal concentration of
the Chinese chess players.

Lost amongst chaotic clatters
I see nature's magnificence
extended from the barrio street
to the silent volcano
adding a puzzling note
to the charged surroundings of Balungao.

Ashok K. Bhargava

Caroline 'Ceri Naz' Nazareno

Carolin 'Ceri' Nazareno

Caroline Nazareno-Gabis a.k.a. Ceri Naz, born in Anda, Pangasinan known as a 'poet of peace and friendship', is a multi-awarded poet, journalist, editor, publicist, linguist, educator, and women's advocate.

Graduated cum laude with the degree of Bachelor of Elementary Education, specialized in General Science at Pangasinan State University. Ceri have been a voracious researcher in various arts, science and literature. She volunteered in Richmond Multicultural Concerns Society, TELUS World Science, Vancouver Art Gallery, and Vancouver Aquarium.

She was privileged to be chosen as one of the Directors of Writers Capital International Foundation (WCIF), Member of the Poetry Posse, one of the Board of Directors of Galaktika ATUNIS Magazine based in Albania; the World Poetry Canada and International Director to Philippines; Global Citizen's Initiatives Member, Association for Women's rights in Development (AWID) and Anacbanua. She has been a 4th Placer in World Union of Poets Poetry Prize 2016, Writers International Network-Canada ''Amazing Poet 2015'', The Frang Bardhi Literary Prize 2014 (Albania), the sair-gazeteci or Poet-Journalist Award 2014 (Tuzla, Istanbul, Turkey) and World Poetry Empowered Poet 2013 (Vancouver, Canada).

Tattoos of Khmer Rouge

Built in ideology
To protect the mystic past,
Empire of the westernized
Have gone into dust,
Oh dear Kampuchea,
Where art thou?
Angels' wings turned radically outcast
From the regime of starved freedom.
Will there be more pleas
To revive million lives
In the verdant utopia?

ang muhon
(Filipino Version The Milestone)

nakagapos
ang mga inipon
at piniling
kalansay
ng alaala

napuspos
ang mga pinagpawisan
at inamag
na pag-asa

nasunog
ang mga sanga
at binakurang
puntod ng pagkakahulma

nalimas na't nalagas
ang pakiramdam
ng huwad na paglaya

isang gabi'y nahipan
ang ilong
nitong lakas
at nagliwanag
ang daliri
ng panahon

kasabay
ang bantayog
ng pagbangon.

the milestone
(English Version)

imprisoned
from the sanctions
and skeletons
of memories

impaired
by demised
and deflated hope

inflamed
branches
of boundaries
and chambers
of mending

far-gone and fallen
contours of passion
and feigned liberty

at the sundown
of a vision
was a breathing nose
of strength
and radiating fingers
of time

the milestone
of the rising.

Lenten prayer

all of the days
we've lived,
we're living,
and we'll be living
we offer to You dear Father...
grant us the love & strength,
the wisdom and compassion,
the peace that we wish,
so we can forgive those
who have caused us enormities...

Carolin 'Ceri' Nazareno

Swapna Behera

Swapna Behera is a bilingual contemporary poet, author, translator and editor from Odisha, India .She was a teacher from 1984 to 2015 . Her stories, poems and articles are widely published in National and International journals, and ezines, and are translated into different national and International languages. She has penned four books. She was conferred upon the Prestigious International Poesis Award of Honor at the 2nd Bharat Award for Literature as Jury in 2015, The Enchanting Muse Award in India World Poetree Festival 2017, World Icon of Peace Award in 2017, and the Pentasi B World Fellow Poet in 2017.. She is the recipient of Gold Cross Of Wisdom Award ,the medal for The Best Teachers of the World from World Union of Poets in 2018, and The LIfe time Achievement Award ,The Best Planner Award, The Sahitya Shiromani Award, ATAL BiHARI BAJPAYEE AWARD 2018, Ambassador De Literature Award 2018 .She is the Ambassador of Humanity by Hafrikan Prince Art World Africa 2018 and an official member of World Nation's Writers Union ,Kazakhstan2018. At present she is the manager at Large, Planner and Columnist of The Literati, the administrator of several poetic groups ,the member of the Special Council of Five of World Union of Poets and the Cultural Ambassador of Inner Child Press U.S.

AA Ka Ma Boi .... The song of the Sadhabas

on the full moon day of Kartik
the great legacy celebrates,
lot of miniature paper boats
made out of cork
banana tree barks
with small oil lamps
reminiscence of sailor's voyage and glory
from kalinga to
Java, Sumatra, Borneo
Once the huge
decorative boats with swan beak heads
the Ajhalas controlling the directions
songs of their gracious wives
echo in the sky
the waves of the Bay of Bengal vibrates
Aaa Ka Ma Boi,
Pana Gua Thoi
Pana Gua tora,
Masaka Dharam More
prayer for their safe return
from turbulence and pirates
offering beetle leaves and nuts
the huge boats sail and sail
months together in deep sea ..
up and down with the winds

Carrying coconut, spices,
salt, cloves, bettlenuts
precious stones and elephants from Kalinga
The women adulate in the shore
for the safe return
Offering beetle leaf and nuts

Art, architecture, dance
songs mingle and zingle of two distant places
the boat sails in the sea ....

today in Odisha the miniature boats
sail in the rivers on this day
to celebrate a legacy and memory

The boats of love sail
 messengers
in the full moon day of Kartik ..

 a lamp burns..........in each boat ....
a lamp burns in each heart ......

~ * ~

Kartik is the name of a month in Hindu calendar
Sadhabas- they were the ancient marine traders of Kalinga
Ajhala; - fabric sails used to harness the wind power to
move the boats
AA - is the first two letters of the month of Aasadha of the
Hindu calendar correspondence to June July
Ka - is the first two letters of Kartika, month of the Hindu
Calendar represents October and November
Ma - is the first two letters of the month of Margashira
Boi - is the first two letters of the month of Boishakha
Kalinga-the ancient name of Odisha, a state in the Eastern
coast of India

Fractured Democracy

when the farmers scream for food
a tiny girl gets stitches
though it never heals
nor kills the rapists

democracy is fractured

when the small boy sings
 the national anthem
peeps through the school window
to get a book and hook mid- day meal

democracy is fractured

when someone ascends on the shoulders
 the ballots become bullets
silence prevails in the courtyard

democracy is fractured

when the river carries the corpse
and cries for pollutions
martyr's widow runs from pillar to post

democracy is fractured

when democracy swings
with hopes and sails on tears
it is fractured

and cries for a plaster!!! .....

A Midnight Deal

December midnight

a deal for a blanket

in the footpath

to save the frozen blood

just a midnight deal

the signature of blood

on her torn frock

simply a deal

in the dark subway

for a blanket!!!

Swapna Behera

Albert 'Infinite' Carrasco

Albert 'Infinite' Carassco

I'm a project life philanthropist, I speak about the non ethical treatment of poor ghetto people. Why? My family was their equal, my great grandmother and great grandfather was poor, my grandmother and grandfather, my mother and father, poverty to my family was a sequel, a traditional Inheritance of the subliminal. I paid attention to the decades of regression, i tried to make change, but when I came to the fork in the road and looked at the signs that read wrong < > right, I chose the left, the wrong direction, because of street life interactions a lot around me met death or incarceration. I failed myself and others. I regret my decisions, I can't reincarnate dead men, but I can give written visions in laymens. I'm back at that fork in the road, instead of it saying wrong or right, I changed it, now it says dead men < > life.

Infinite poetry @lulu.com

Alcarrasco2 on YouTube

Infinite the poet on reverbnation

Infinite Poetry

http://www.lulu.com/us/en/shop/al-infinite-carrasco/infinite-poetry/paperback/product-21040240.html

Southeast Asia

Eleven countries of paradise
Tropical jungles and beaches will definitely entice.
Beautiful copper and bronze statues,
Mountaintops have jaw dropping views.
Man, woman and children merchants are all over,
selling fruit, vegetables rice and noodles.
All of the Palaces and temples are incredible.
Monks in prayer sending blessing throughout the
atmosphere.
Most of the languages are... Khmer
Lao, Thai, Burmese, Tagalog, Malay, Indonesian and
Vietnamese.
The place I speak of is Southeast Asia, once called the East
Indies.

Gunshots

The sounds of gunshots excited me, growing up in the hood I heard em daily, to me it was a sign of power, I was young, I wasn't equating the sound with bodily harm or murder. Blam blam blam I would run to the window to look at the shooter, then admire that ghetto soldier, Light then sound, light then sound, lightening then thunder round after round, I wished I could've been closer. I wanted to be like those guys, I wanted a gun so I could feel the power while hearing the sound as I pulled the trigger aiming at the sky. I felt as if those guys were untouchable, everybody ran from them if they were able, they were my idols. I couldn't wait for the next time to hear the ghetto echo! I grew up. I became the one being watched by some young sons that have my old fascination, they love the sound and power, when they saw me, they idolized a ghetto soldier, just like me they don't understand that when they saw the light and heard the sound, it was an attempt or murder. I wish I could explain the cause and effect but I can't because what excited me made me a lifer.

Urban poetry

My poetry derives from poverty, drugs guns, cold bodies and teary eyes. As a youngen my dreams got side tracked when my father got sent back. I wanted to be in the military, I would've enlisted after high school and been a soldier like many other men in my family. I knew that'll get me out the hood, combat boots, camo and a dog chain bearing my name, I would've looked good. Life became fubar, fucked up beyond all repair, I wound up in the concrete trenches, day and night you saw me out there. Still young and naive I became an armed force like the army, navy, air force and marines, had my deuce power and understanding build cipher amongst other protection while chasing the almighty dollar. I missed the opportunity to be a kid that grew to become a man that got married on a base and raised military brats because I was trapped making profit off cooked coke packs. It was instant rebellion, I wanted to feed my mother and brothers, At that time I wasn't trying to build a business or reach a million, I just wanted to maintain the lifestyle we lived when pops was liv'n. We wasn't rich but we weren't poor either, life took a bad turn by us losing the breadwinner. Things got ugly with no one to guide me, so I moved in the direction of blood money. Soon after I understood that terminology. Slugs pricked skin and mangled anatomy... hood phlebotomy. Not all currency had red stains because blood didn't reach pockets when shot in the brain, so it remained dirty green in a murderous game, Lost most of my team for turning pure coke into crack cocaine.

Eliza Segiet

After earning a Master's Degree in Philosophy at the Jagiellonian University in Krakaw, Poland, Eliza Segiet proceeded with her post-graduate studies in the fields of Cultural Knowledge, Penal Revenue and Economic Criminal Law, Arts and Literature and Film and Television Production in the Polish city, Lodz.

With specific regard to her creative writings, the author describes herself as being torn in her passion for engaging in two literary genres: Poetry and Drama. A similar dichotomy from within is reflected on Segiet's own words about her true nature: She likes to look at the clouds, but she keeps both of her feet set firmly on the ground.

The author describes her worldview as being in harmony with that of Arthur Schopenhauer: "Ordinary people merely think how they shall 'spend' their time; a man of talent tries to 'use' it".

Eliza Segiet

Echo

On the rocky walls,
suspended coffins.
Long ago mourned
they connect
the past with the present.

Prepared
for the soul to be closer to heaven?
Awarded for a good life?
Maybe just to
give them silence and peace
when they themselves are silent?

In the Echo valley
still are alive
the sounds of history.

Prepared
for remembrance
they hang
not to delight.

But to amaze!

Translated by Artur Komoter

Moss

At dawn she visited a neighbour
– the one on the second floor,
and she only sighed:
not just yet, I don't want to, I have to…
She did not finish.

On the sinuous, unstable
—like life—stairs
they went together
to where the earth
can give birth
– only to moss.

Translated by Artur Komoter

I Will Be While I Am

Eve was first,
and I?

I'm like the sun,
which blings –
real, yet elusive.

On the surface of eternity
man is only a flash.

She was and is,
I –
will be while I am.

Translated by Artur Komoter

William S. Peters Sr.

Bill's writing career spans a period of over 50 years. Being first Published in 1972, Bill has since went on to Author in excess of 40 additional Volumes of Poetry, Short Stories, etc., expressing his thoughts on matters of the Heart, Spirit, Consciousness and Humanity. His primary focus is that of Love, Peace and Understanding!

Bill says . . .

I have always likened Life to that of a Garden. So, for me, Life is simply about the Seeds we Sow and Nourish. All things we "Think and Do", will "Be" Cause and eventually manifest itself to being an "Effect" within our own personal "Existences" and "Experiences" . . . whether it be Fruit, Flowers, Weeds or Barren Landscapes! Bill highly regards the Fruits of his Labor and wishes that everyone would thus go on to plant "Lovely" Seeds on "Good Ground" in their own Gardens of Life!

to connect with Bill, he is all things Inner Child

www.iaminnerchild.com

Personal Web Site

www.iamjustbill.com

And we listen

Our lives were simple,
Our boats took to the waters
And fed our families,
And the villages of our dreams,
And of our hearts

We practiced community
And cooperation
With one and another

Life is simple,
You take what the Mother
Of all things yields
And offer in return
Your gratefulness

Our 'Holy'
Is to be found
In the connections,
That betwixt
The Land,
The Waters
And the Skies

We are a reverent people
Who honor the sacrifices
And ongoing presence
Of our ancestors

The waters speak to us,
And we listen
just as they spoke
To our Fathers before us

The Earth, Mother
Speaks as well,
And we listen

The Winds and the Skies, and the Clouds too
Speak to us
And we listen

Ellis

With his fingers digging in the soil,
He felt immersed in a certain reverence
That exuded the meaning of life

He was a simple man,
With simple needs,
He did not seem to want much ...

I am sure like most of us
He also had dreams ... such as,
Time to sit in his rocking chair,
Smoke his corn-cob pipe,
And maybe play a little guitar
While sitting out in the front yard
Under the tall majestic Pine trees
He had planted
Decades ago

Maybe Nana would darn his socks,
And fix one of his favorite meals ...
Stewed chicken

Other dreams were such things as,
A new roof on the shed,
Before,
The planting of the spring seed...
Seeing them break through their furrows,
Which meant ...
Growth,
Budding and blossoming,
And a fruitful harvest
To come ...

As long as he
Nurtured,
Watered,
And weeded,
His garden.

He was a simple man...

Yes ....

He was a simple man,
With simple needs,
He did not seem to want much ...

He was my grandfather... Ellis

Nurture my mind

Feed me
Feed the world

Give me a school
Give me a classroom
Give me a teacher
Give me a book
Give me the opportunity
For my mind to expand
Into the beyond

I wish to discover my horizon
Where the possibilities of my potential
Have made a place for me
And await my arrival

I am a poem of humanity
Waiting to be written

I am a song of creation,
Let us dance,
Let us sing ....
Together

Give me a school
Give me a classroom
Give me a teacher
Give me a book
Give me the opportunity
For my mind to expand
Into the beyond

Give me a pen
And a piece of paper
I will share with you
Some of the thoughts
From my soul

Nurture my mind
Feed me
Feed the world

William S. Peters, Sr.

May

2019

Features

~ * ~

Emad Al-Haydary

Hussein Nasser Jabr

Wahab Sheriff

Abdul Razzaq Al Ameeri

i Fly

because I Can

... said the Dreamer to the world.

www.iamjustbill.com

Emad
Al-Haydary

Emad Al-Haydary

Emad Al-Haydary he is a poet and Teacher of Arabic language from Iraq porn 1970 in Najaf, he has M.A. in Arabic Literature, he did published 4th poetry books : (Shades That Do Not Like Ash 1999), (Prayers of Remission 2007) , (Talking To Her in Heaven 2008), (Celebrating My Death... Suggesting a Panting Life and a one novel (Sons of Sins), he is a member of Iraqi Union of Writers.ters.

Relaxing

To my teacher
Sitting in the end of her life
I want you to know that I'm relaxing now,
like a shadow tired of following the Sun
like a butterfly full with joy.
I was melting like an orphan boy hiding from the eyes of
strangers.
When I looked from the hole of the exile wall,
I saw my home hanged
I don't have any other way
Just to come back to you,
My teacher
And listen to you when you are singing -- my home my
home.

Translated by Faleeha Hassan

Meeting

The star was tired of Shining at nights

And I was tired of sitting in nothing.

When we did meet,

The stars of noon were born.

Translated by Faleeha Hassan

Worthy To Be Dreamt Of

With two dewy eyes
And two eyelids like the wings of a butterfly
I pick up the color of the dawn
Stealthily, away from the night's eyes
Doing the ceremonies of my single dream
Here is the map of innocence
That is a field replete with the spring
I wonder where I am
Apparently, (my kingdom is not here in this world)
Searching I am for a mystery hidden in the ports
At which they'll return to their dancing waves
Cutting short an age that doesn't respond
to warmth at a moment of ecstasy,
A desire in me may have trodden my bones
Or it might be a wish to kiss the waves of the sea
Or it could be my body travelling
through an old mountain love
Water is a nymph that does not know what desertion is
Meadows are verses recited by heaven
That is my beloved's face
I wonder where I am
And you who's sitting in the distance of a cloud from me
With love coming between us
At a gate with no smell of bullets
How to get to you my sparrow
Resting on the road of love
Don't make of me, where the stars meet
An erotic tale talked to the infatuated lovers
This is the echo of my questions saying:
It's your nest that you're dreaming of
Then I cry, (my kingdom is not here in this world)
Water has colored the poem

Meadows make a color chanted for the world
That is my beloved's face: There's an echo there
It's your nest you're dreaming of
Nothing is worthy being dreamt of but you
O, charming peace

Translated by Hussein Nasse

Emad Al-Haydary

Hussein
Nasser
Jabr

\

Hussein Nasser Jabr , he is a Poet & translator , he has M.A. in English Linguistics 2006, Born in Nasiriya near to the ancient city of Ur, south of Iraq, in 1964; lives in Najaf, 180 km south of Baghdad. A multi-task person; works as: CERTIFIED HIGH SCHOOL TEACHER (Official Teacher) University Lecturer (Part-time Faculty member), Certified translator (to and from English). Literary translator (especially poetry), published English poems in Iraq and abroad, in books, magazines and bulletins. As a translator, published translations of six books, in English and Arabic, in addition to a variety of non-literary translations of research papers.

To Baghdad Passing by the Sun

(1)

Slow to Depart
Mirrors, beyond my eyes, I crushed
Yesterday was just a fleeting moment
Today is more severe
Than the scars on the skin
in which I hide
Pale was what remained of me, and
Fast what'd past of my age
Glory to the successive moments
We are all passing away
Unnoticed
Though slow to depart

(2)

Under the Rain
We shall meet there in the winter
At the rail station...in Baghdad:
Two strange sparrows-
Wet and shivering under the rain-
Migrated from the farthest south
To be left there, nestless
We've lost our home and all the addresses
of our friends
There remained alone, Known to no one but the rain

(3)

The Sun
For not to be celled
The sun rounds its face-

Imprisoned; yet, in its light
But, when released
Colorless eyes it becomes
Burning with darkling core
Devouring its light buds
When will you be, O, Sun
As in the dreams of those
Who own no overcoats?

A Soliloquy Divine at the Holy Sanctuary

Along the way
No distance is there
Between you and me.
Curtains of light are off,
Illusions melt,
Our steps entangle
And then we are one.
Unaware of my wake,
I longingly fly
Into the lap of God
Floating on the wave of love.
Silently sending looks away
Trembling but standing still
My stature flows away.
Hopefully shall I, if go beyond
The realm of love
be a shade of God.

O, Golden World

How warm and loved.
Get up anon, it's already morn:
Plains are tickling their jungle
Mounts are embracing the snow.
Mounds are a velvet soft
Woven with a scented moon.
O, you! A forest of dew
whose lakes are roaming
Like girls blooming
With eyes caught in whispering sleep.
And in the fire of man
Light and flare.
You immortal blaze!
For your sun,
Get your morning horses saddled
On whose faces
A white star of hope.
O, precious world!
Your seas are a giant pearl
Whose shell is your flashing eyelid
And in whose secret are wishes stored.

Hussein Nasser Jabr

Wahab Sheriff

Wahab Sheriff is a poet born in Najaf / Iraq on 04/03/1961,

He is the editor of the cultural magazine Almnhal, he has
B.Sc. Journalism / Media from University of Baghdad ,
and he is a member of the Peace and Solidarity Council.
Mr. Sheriff won many Arabic Poetry Prize in Iraq , and he
published nineteen poetry books.

Good for me

Good for me to laugh to the early morning,
wet by children
Whispering to one another:
"That one is laughing like vacancy between teeth
Like our cooked naivety, that is laughing
and this...."
As if the municipality felt sympathy for the sparrows of the
town,
the lamp stared onto our agonies in the house yard, and
naughtiness of excited boys.
That one is laughing of horrible losses haunting him,
of how hard he'd already died.
Good for me to feel angry among the lines of tears.
With all oppression of snobs,
Haven't my eyelashes felt injustice, and smeared dreams?
Good for me to use up my sadness's rivers one by one,
So that the night would be full of satisfied pleasing cats.
Good for me to hunt my temptations from one country to
another,
For my shirt to be just a part of me,
To be myself in the unknown
To grow a spike for the lovers stricken by white hair,
Good for me to read in my sadness book
what to come of pain and various experiences
Good for me to be understood by someone
who claps when I cut myself up,
Good for me to throw my tires into the river,
For I know who would suck the sorrow of my age.
And never lie down but at his sweetest follies.

Transited by Hussein Nasser Jabr

Poet

You can't stay alone

At least you need a frog' sound to protest against you

You need a blue bird to kiss your cheek in morning

You need a blooming bud which can take you from all of to

you.

Translated by Faleeha Hassan

Fact

There are no cities can avoid those whose in love with her

There are no villages that lionize the deceivers

And the first will die , the one he lost the truth

Translated by Faleeha Hassan

Abdul Razzaq Al Ameeri

Abdul Razzaq Al Ameeri (1947-2010)
He held a BA in Islamic Jurisprudence. He was a member of the Union of Writes of Iraq. He did wrote two collections of Poetry:
- Oblation of the Twentieth Century in 1969
- Diaries of the Permanent Question in 2010

The Game and the Deluge.

O, lady !
Your face is a word
Hidden under the feathers of a peacock,
A lady in a large hall .. alone
Whose secret is wrapped in nothingness.
O, lady !
I avoid crying
Beyond my occult voice
While repeating the words of a sentence.
My fear cancels off all things
To keep you a lady of the absolute
Reducing this paper cosmos
To an idol on a banquet of the earth
Announcing the death of Man.
 The game could not stop the deluge.

The River of a Knife

Poetry is ritualistic
O, you, my wish
Be goddesses and amulets
Or keep silent for ever.
And turn off as a dream
In the head of a castaway,
A banquet of fruits for the spirit,
Crows 're hiding the oblation love
In a river of a knife.

All are a Chatter Bag

All are a bag of cackles,
All travel throughout words
Drawing the circle of death.
Black magic
Declares the world as my grave.
Death is the road of gnostic.
So be steps and follow my steps
The path of God passes through
the sins of the exiles.
By Abdul Razzaq Al Ameeri
Translated by Hussein Nasser Jabr

Remembering

our fallen soldiers of verse

Janet Perkins Caldwell
February 14, 1959 ~ September 20, 2016

Alan W. Jankowski
16 March 1961 ~ 10 March 2017

Inner Child Press
News

We are so excited to share and announce a few of the current books, as well as the new and upcoming books of some of our Poetry Posse authors.

On the following pages we present to you ...

Jackie Davis Allen

Gail Weston Shazor

hülya n. yılmaz

Nizar Sartawi

Faleeha Hassan

Fahredin Shehu

Caroline 'Ceri' Nazareno

Eliza Segiet

William S. Peters, Sr.

Now Available at

www.innerchildpress.com

No Illusions

Through the Looking Glass

Jackie Davis Allen

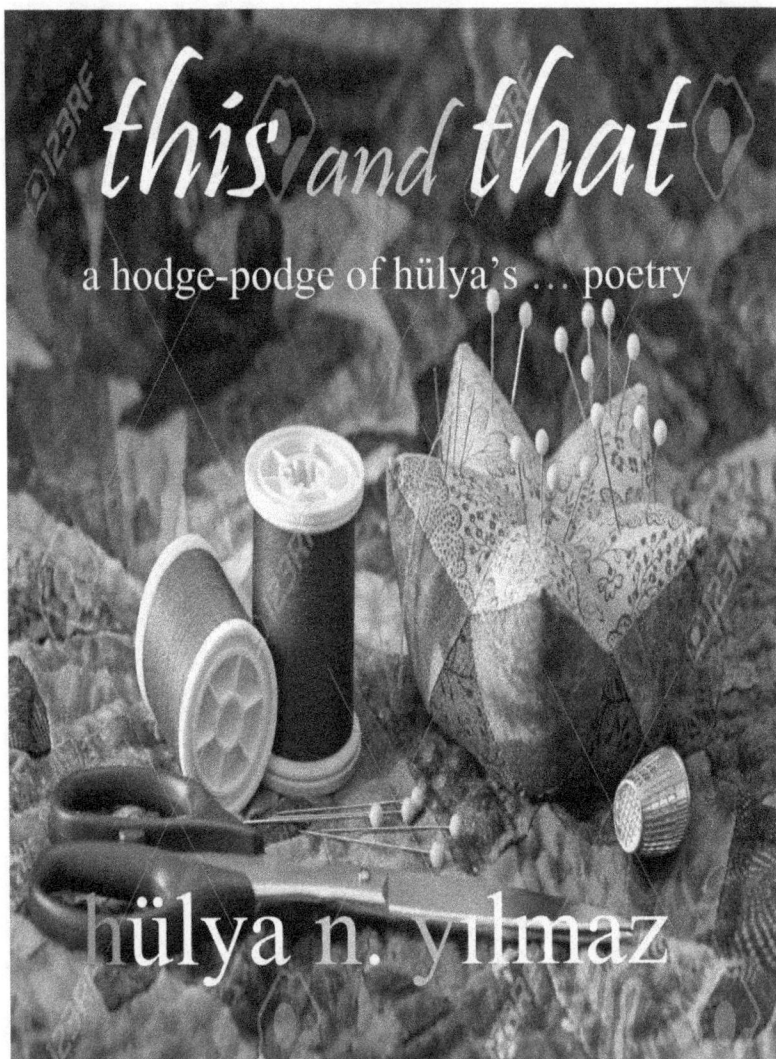

this and that

a hodge-podge of hülya's ... poetry

hülya n. yılmaz

Now Available at
www.innerchildpress.com

HERENOW

◆

FAHREDIN SHEHU

Now Available at
www.innerchildpress.com

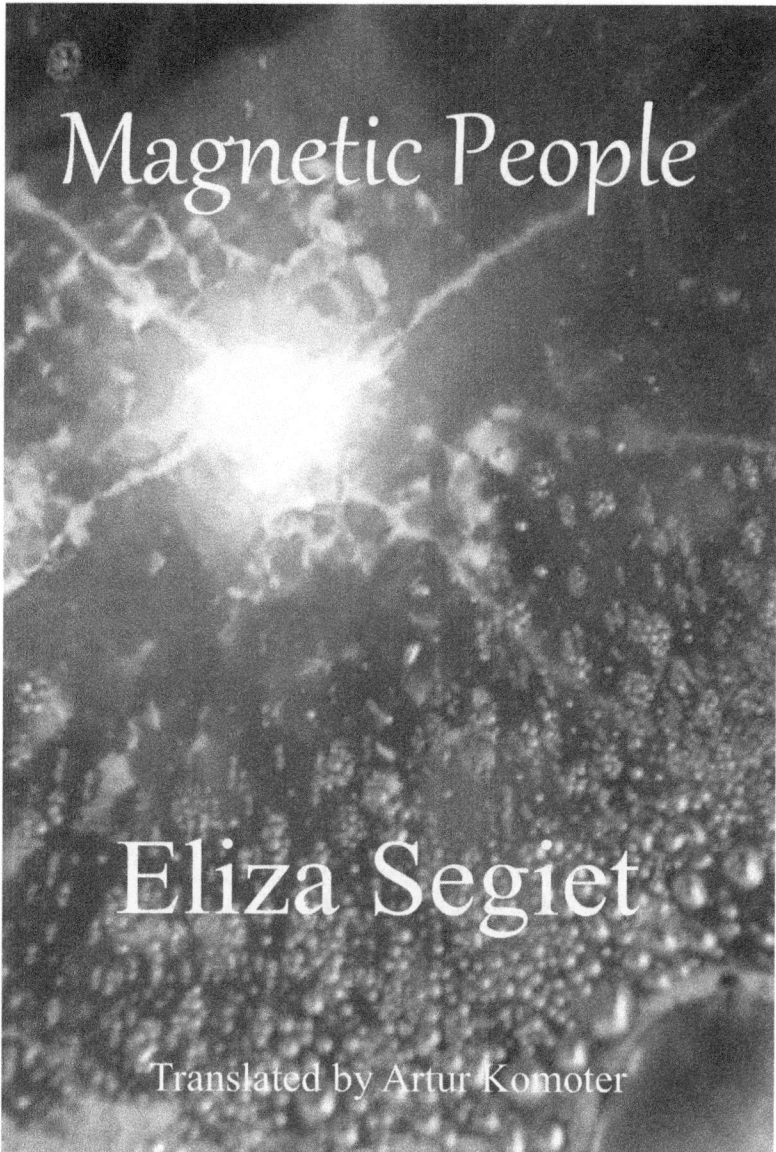

Magnetic People

Eliza Segiet

Translated by Artur Komoter

Now Available at
www.innerchildpress.com

Now Available at
www.innerchildpress.com

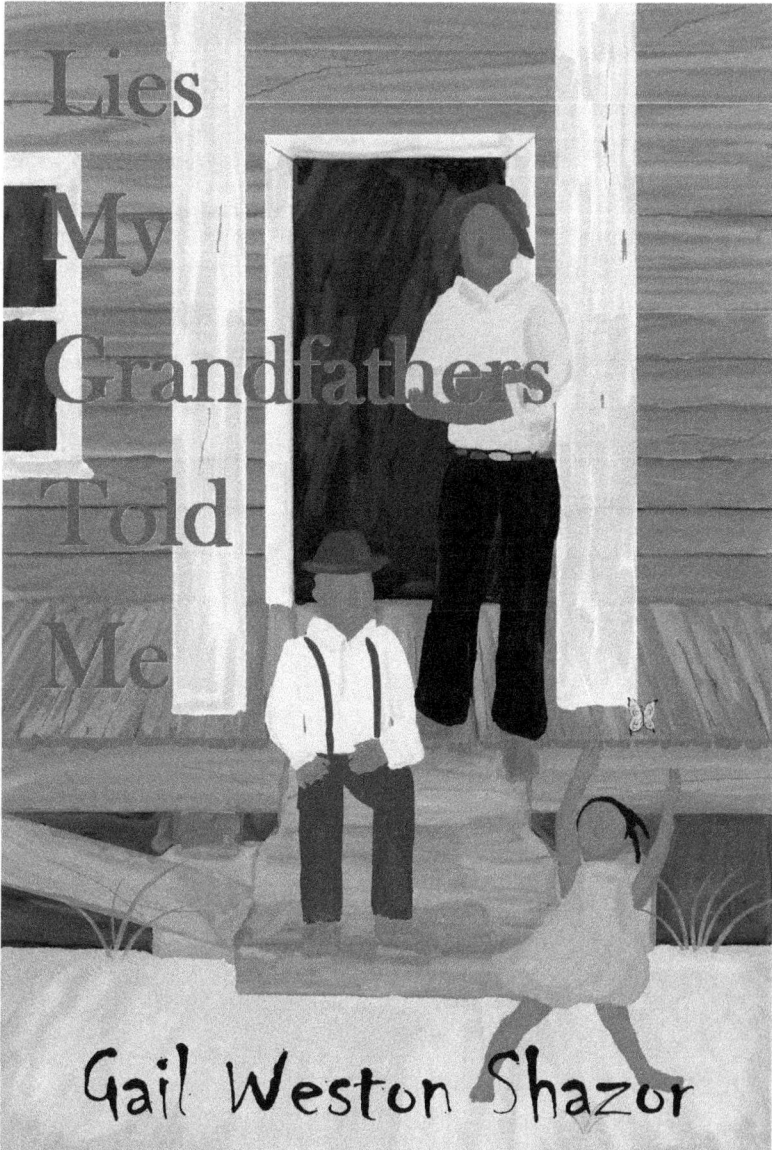

Lies
My
Grandfathers
Told
Me

Gail Weston Shazor

Now Available at
www.innerchildpress.com

Aflame

Memoirs in Verse

hülya n. yılmaz

Now Available at
www.innerchildpress.com

My Shadow

Nizar Sartawi

Mass Graves

Faleeha Hassan

Now Available at
www.innerchildpress.com

Breakfast

for

Butterflies

Faleeha Hassan

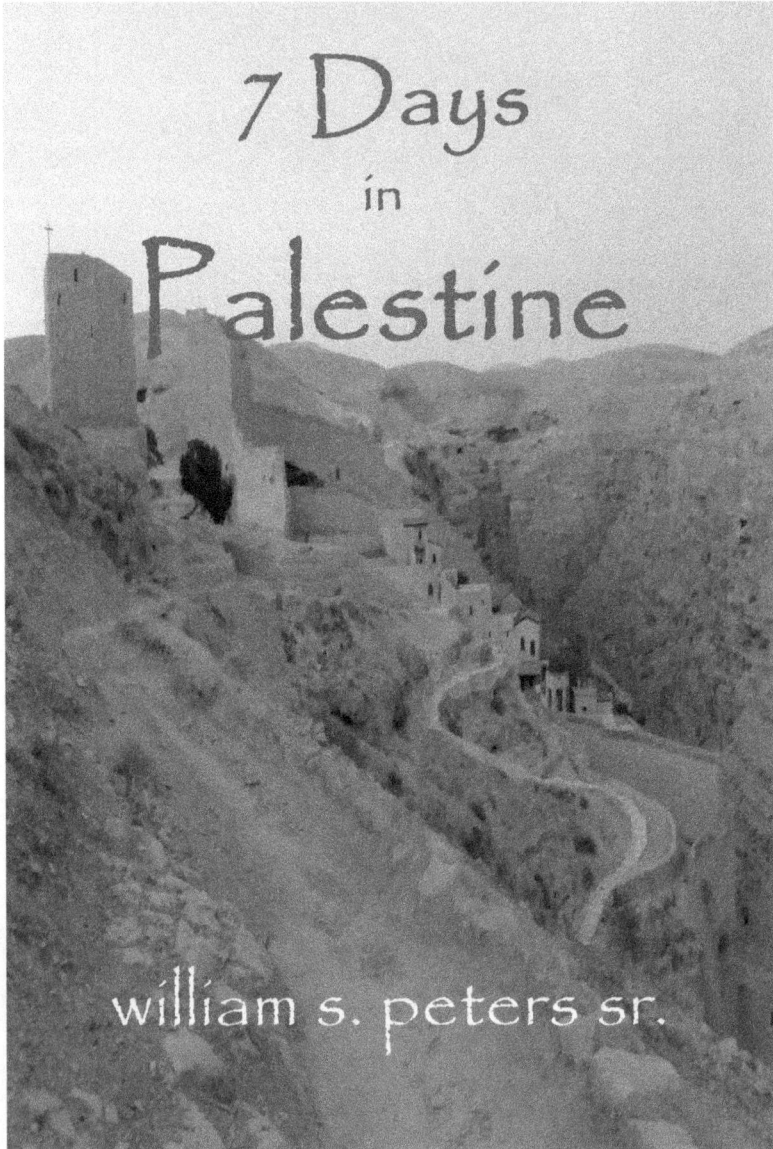

The Year of the Poet VI ~ May 2019

Now Available at
www.innerchildpress.com

inner child press
presents

Tunisia My Love

william s. peters, sr.

163

Coming in the Summer of 2019

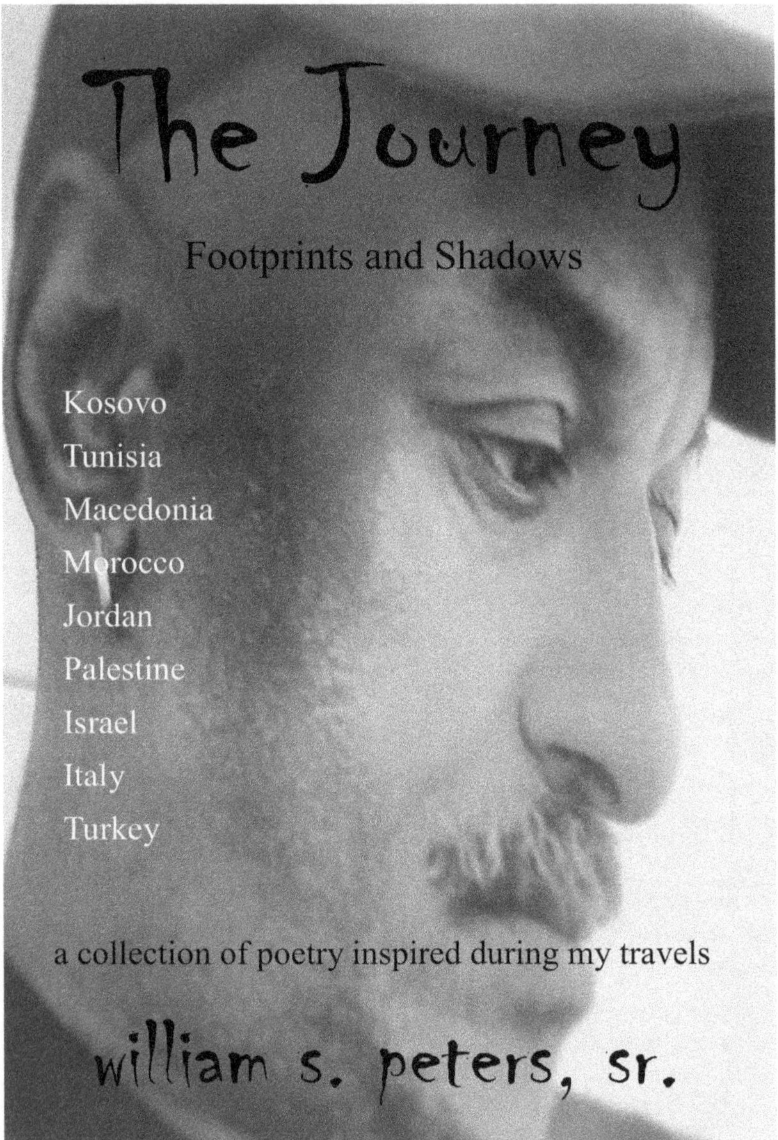

The Journey

Footprints and Shadows

Kosovo

Tunisia

Macedonia

Morocco

Jordan

Palestine

Israel

Italy

Turkey

a collection of poetry inspired during my travels

william s. peters, sr.

Now Available at
www.innerchildpress.com

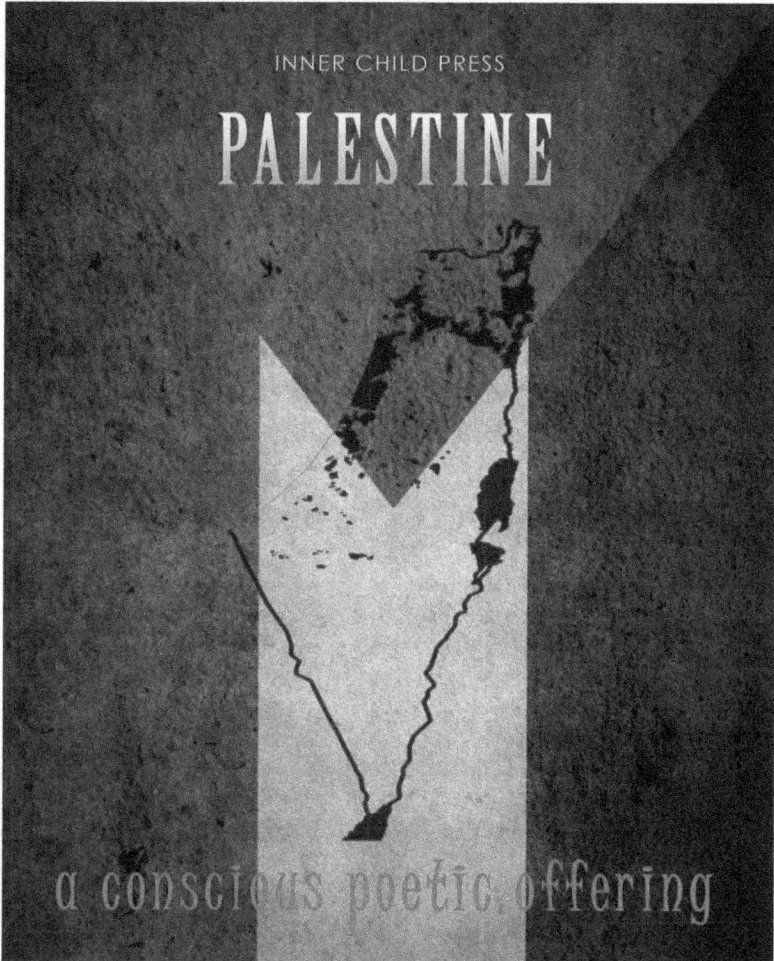

Now Available at
www.innerchildpress.com

INNER CHILD PRESS

THIS IS WHY I
SLEEP

william s. peters sr.

Now Available at
www.innerchildpress.com

Think on These Things
Book II

william s. peters, sr.

Now Available at
www.innerchildpress.com

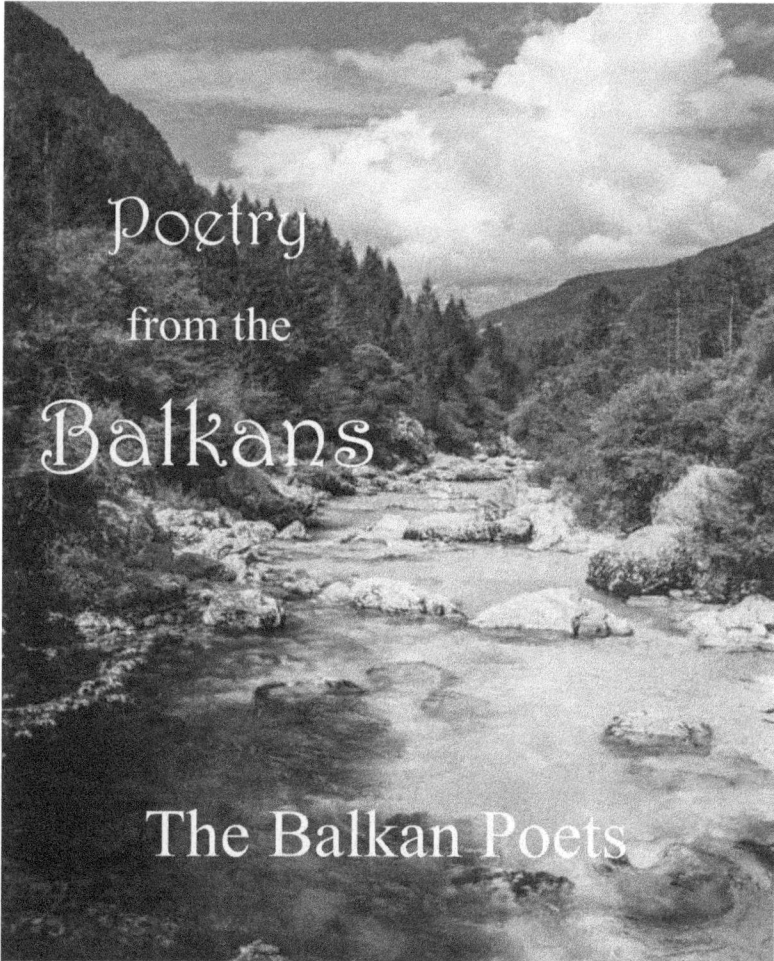

Poetry
from the
Balkans

The Balkan Poets

Other

Anthological

works from

Inner Child Press International

www.innerchildpress.com

Inner Child Press International
presents

A Love Anthology
2019

The Love Poets

Now Available

www.worldhealingworldpeacepoetry.com

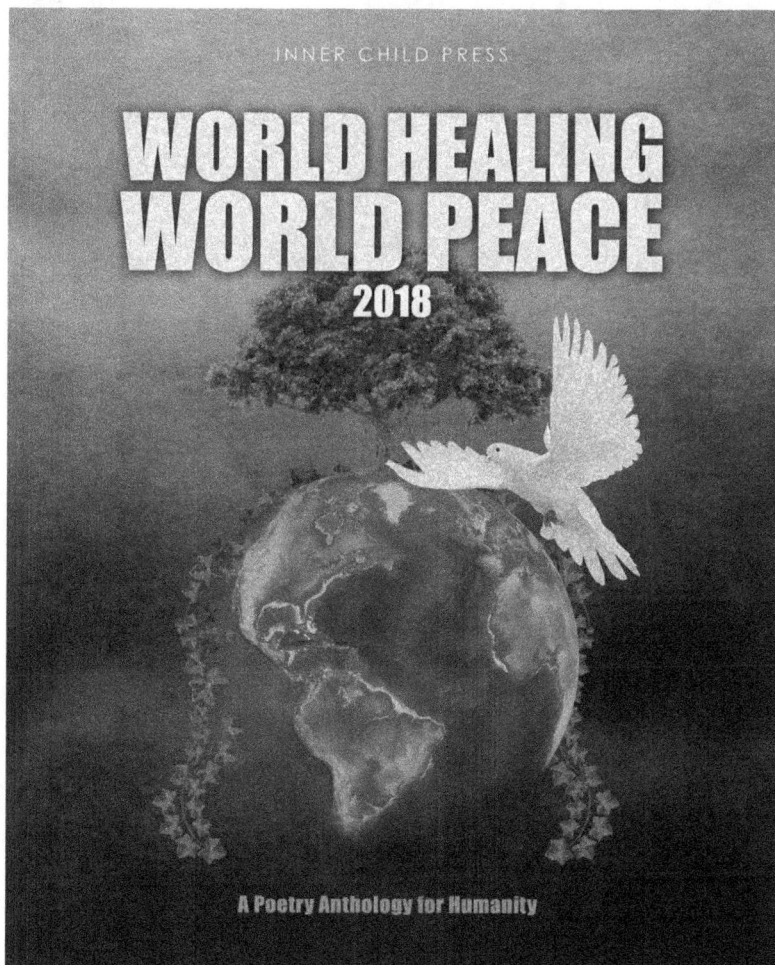

INNER CHILD PRESS

WORLD HEALING
WORLD PEACE
2018

A Poetry Anthology for Humanity

Now Available

www.worldhealingworldpeacepoetry.com

Now Available

www.worldhealingworldpeacepoetry.com

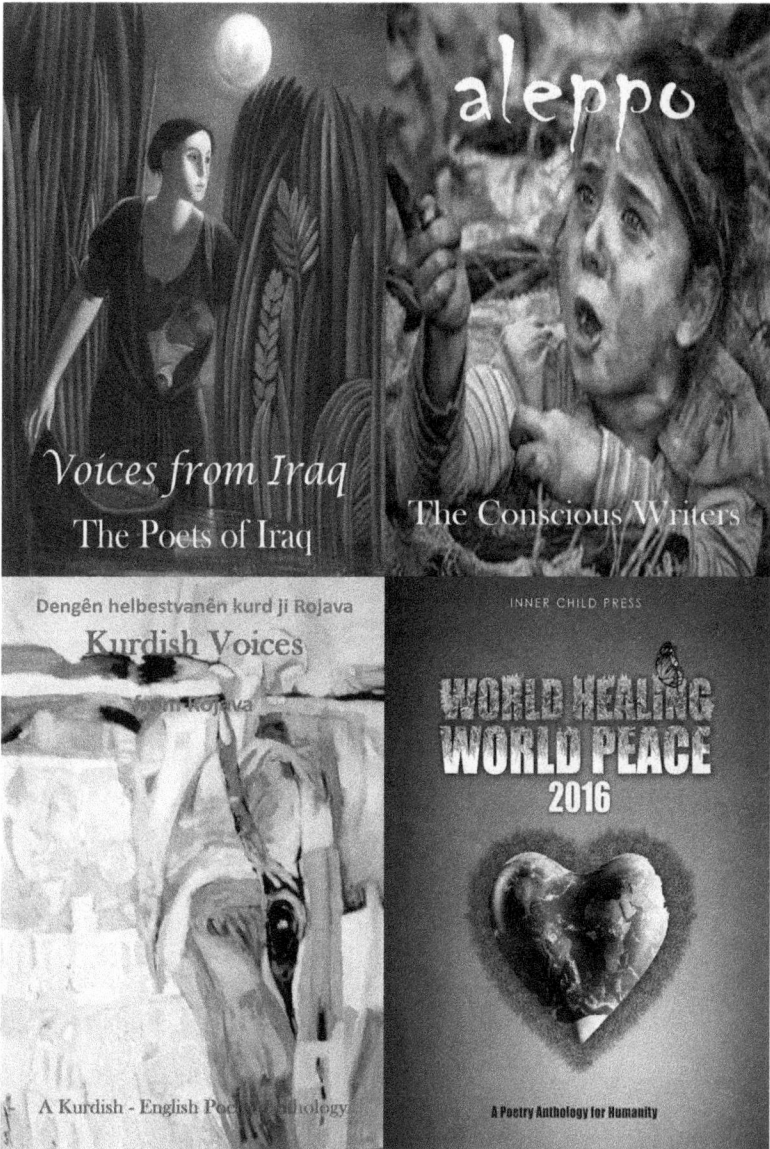

Now Available

www.innerchildpress.com/anthologies

Now Available

www.innerchildpress.com/anthologies

Janet
gone too soon . . .

healing through words

Poetry ... Prose ... Prayer ... Stories

a
Poetically
Spoken
Anthology
volume I
Collector's Edition

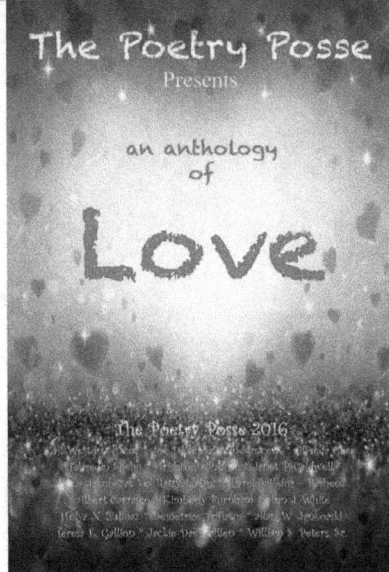

The Poetry Posse
Presents

an anthology
of

Love

The Poetry Posse 2016

Now Available

www.innerchildpress.com/anthologies

want my

a collection of the Voices of Many inspired by . . .

Monte Smith

Monte Smith

want my

to . . .

volume II

to . . .   volume 3

a collection of the Voices of Many inspired by . . .

Monte Smith

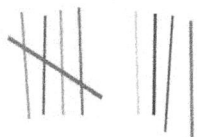

(9 lines . . .)

for those who are challenged

an anthology of Poetry inspired by . . .

Poetry Dancer

Now Available

www.innerchildpress.com/anthologies

The Year of the Poet
January 2014

The Poetry Posse

Jamie Bond
Gail Weston Shazor
Albert 'Infinite' Carrasco
Siddartha Beth Pierce
Janet P. Caldwell
June 'Bugg' Barefield
Debbie M. Allen
Tony Henninger
Joe DaVerbal Minddancer
Robert Gibbons
Neetu Wali
Shareef Abdur-Rasheed
William S. Peters, Sr.

Carnation

Our January Feature
Terri L. Johnson

the Year of the Poet
February 2014

violets

The Poetry Posse

Jamie Bond
Gail Weston Shazor
Albert 'Infinite' Carrasco
Siddartha Beth Pierce
Janet P. Caldwell
June 'Bugg' Barefield
Debbie M. Allen
Tony Henninger
Joe DaVerbal Minddancer
Robert Gibbons
Neetu Wali
Shareef Abdur-Rasheed
William S. Peters, Sr.

Our February Features
Teresa E. Gallion & Robert Gibson

the Year of the Poet
March 2014

The Poetry Posse
Jamie Bond
Gail Weston Shazor
Albert 'Infinite' Carrasco
Siddartha Beth Pierce
Janet P. Caldwell
June 'Bugg' Barefield
Debbie M. Allen
Tony Henninger
Joe DaVerbal Minddancer
Robert Gibbons
Neetu Wali
Shareef Abdur-Rasheed
Kimberly Burnham
William S. Peters, Sr.

daffodil

Our March Featured Poets
Alicia C. Cooper & hülya yılmaz

the Year of the Poet
April 2014

The Poetry Posse
Jamie Bond
Gail Weston Shazor
Albert 'Infinite' Carrasco
Siddartha Beth Pierce
Janet P. Caldwell
June 'Bugg' Barefield
Debbie M. Allen
Tony Henninger
Joe DaVerbal Minddancer
Robert Gibbons
Neetu Wali
Shareef Abdur-Rasheed
Kimberly Burnham
William S. Peters, Sr.

Our April Featured Poets
Fahredin Shehu
Martina Reisz Newberry
Justin Blackburn
Monte Smith

Sweet Pea

celebrating International poetry month

Now Available

www.innerchildpress.com/the-year-of-the-poet

the year of the poet
May 2014

May's Featured Poets
ReeCee
Joski the Poet
Shannon Stanton

Dedicated To our Children

The Poetry Posse
Jamie Bond
Gail Weston Shazor
Albert 'Infinite' Carrasco
Nakhantu Beth Pierce
Janet P. Caldwell
June 'Bugg' Barefield
Debbie M. Allen
Tony Henninger
Joe DaVerbal Minddancer
Robert Gibbons
Neetu Wali
Shareef Abdur-Rasheed
Kimberly Burnham
William S. Peters, Sr.

Lily of the Valley

the Year of the Poet
June 2014

Love & Relationship

Rose

June's Featured Poets
Shantelle McLin
Jacqueline D. E. Kennedy
Abraham N. Benjamin

The Poetry Posse
Jamie Bond
Gail Weston Shazor
Albert 'Infinite' Carrasco
Siddartha Beth Pierce
Janet P. Caldwell
June 'Bugg' Barefield
Debbie M. Allen
Tony Henninger
Joe DaVerbal Minddancer
Robert Gibbons
Neetu Wali
Shareef Abdur-Rasheed
Kimberly Burnham
William S. Peters, Sr.

The Year of the Poet
July 2014

July Feature Poets
Christena A. V. Williams
Dr. John R. Strum
Rolade Olanrewaju Freedom

The Poetry Posse
Jamie Bond
Gail Weston Shazor
Albert 'Infinite' Carrasco
Siddartha Beth Pierce
Janet P. Caldwell
June 'Bugg' Barefield
Debbie M. Allen
Tony Henninger
Joe DaVerbal Minddancer
Robert Gibbons
Neetu Wali
Shareef Abdur-Rasheed
Kimberly Burnham
William S. Peters, Sr.

Lotus
Asian Flower of the Month

The Year of the Poet
August 2014

Gladiolus

The Poetry Posse
Jamie Bond
Gail Weston Shazor
Albert 'Infinite' Carrasco
Siddartha Beth Pierce
Janet P. Caldwell
June 'Bugg' Barefield
Debbie M. Allen
Tony Henninger
Joe DaVerbal Minddancer
Robert Gibbons
Neetu Wali
Shareef Abdur-Rasheed
Kimberly Burnham
William S. Peters, Sr.

August Feature Poets
Ann White * Rosalind Cherry * Sheila Jenkins

Now Available

www.innerchildpress.com/the-year-of-the-poet

181

The Year of the Poet

September 2014

Aster — Morning-Glory

Wild Chicory September Birthday Flower

September Feature Poets
Florence Malone * Keith Alan Hamilton

The Poetry Posse

Jamie Bond * Gail Weston Shazor * Albert 'Infinite' Carrasco * Siddartha Beth Pierce
Janet P. Caldwell * June 'Bugg' Barefield * Debbie M. Allen * Tony Henninger
Joe DaVerbal Minddancer * Robert Gibbons * Neetu Wali * Shareef Abdur-Rasheed
Kimberly Burnham * William S. Peters, Sr.

THE YEAR OF THE POET

October 2014

Red Poppy

The Poetry Posse

Jamie Bond * Gail Weston Shazor * Albert 'Infinite' Carrasco * Siddartha Beth Pierce
Janet P. Caldwell * June 'Bugg' Barefield * Debbie M. Allen * Tony Henninger
Joe DaVerbal Minddancer * Robert Gibbons * Neetu Wali * Shareef Abdur-Rasheed
Kimberly Burnham * William S. Peters, Sr.

October Feature Poets
Ceri Naz * Rajendra Padhi * Elizabeth Castillo

THE YEAR OF THE POET

November 2014

Chrysanthemum

The Poetry Posse

Jamie Bond * Gail Weston Shazor * Albert 'Infinite' Carrasco * Siddartha Beth Pierce
Janet P. Caldwell * June 'Bugg' Barefield * Debbie M. Allen * Tony Henninger
Joe DaVerbal Minddancer * Robert Gibbons * Neetu Wali * Shareef Abdur-Rasheed
Kimberly Burnham * William S. Peters, Sr.

November Feature Poets
Jocelyn Mosman * Jackie Allen * James Moore * Neville Hiatt

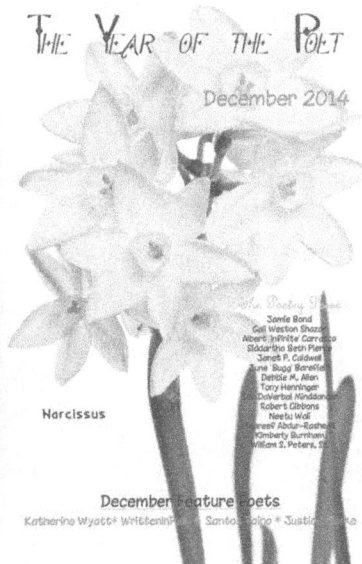

THE YEAR OF THE POET

December 2014

The Poetry Posse
Jamie Bond
Gail Weston Shazor
Albert 'Infinite' Carrasco
Siddartha Beth Pierce
Janet P. Caldwell
June 'Bugg' Barefield
Debbie M. Allen
Tony Henninger
DaVerbal Minddancer
Robert Gibbons
Neetu Wali
Shareef Abdur-Rasheed
Kimberly Burnham
William S. Peters, Sr.

Narcissus

December Feature Poets
Katherine Wyatt * WrittenInk * Santash John * Justin Blake

Now Available

www.innerchildpress.com/the-year-of-the-poet

182

THE YEAR OF THE POET II
January 2015

Garnet

The Poetry Posse

Jamie Bond
Gail Weston Shazor
Albert 'Infinite' Carrasco
Siddartha Beth Pierce
Janet P. Caldwell
Tony Henninger
Joe DaVerbal Minddancer
Robert Gibbons
Neetu Wali
Shareef Abdur - Rasheed
Kimberly Burnham
Ann White
Keith Alan Hamilton
Katherine Wyatt
Fahredin Shehu
Hülya N. Yılmaz
Teresa E. Gallion
Jackie Allen
William S. Peters, Sr.

January Feature Poets
Bismay Mohanti * Jen Walls * Eric Judah

THE YEAR OF THE POET II
February 2015

Amethyst

THE POETRY POSSE

Jamie Bond
Gail Weston Shazor
Albert 'Infinite' Carrasco
Siddartha Beth Pierce
Janet P. Caldwell
Tony Henninger
Joe DaVerbal Minddancer
Robert Gibbons
Neetu Wali
Shareef Abdur - Rasheed
Kimberly Burnham
Ann White
Keith Alan Hamilton
Katherine Wyatt
Fahredin Shehu
Hülya N. Yılmaz
Teresa E. Gallion
Jackie Allen
William S. Peters, Sr.

FEBRUARY FEATURE POETS
Iram Fatima * Bob McNeil * Kerstin Centervall

The Year of the Poet II
March 2015

Our Featured Poets
Heung Sook * Anthony Arnold * Alicia Poland

Bloodstone

The Poetry Posse 2015
Jamie Bond * Gail Weston Shazor * Albert 'Infinite' Carrasco
Siddartha Beth Pierce * Janet P. Caldwell * Tony Henninger
Joe DaVerbal Minddancer * Neetu Wali * Shareef Abdur – Rasheed
Kimberly Burnham * Ann White * Keith Alan Hamilton
Katherine Wyatt * Fahredin Shehu * Hülya N. Yılmaz
Teresa E. Gallion * Jackie Allen * William S. Peters, Sr.

The Year of the Poet II
April 2015

Celebrating International Poetry Month

Our Featured Poets
Raja Williams * Dennis Ferado * Laure Charazac

Diamonds

The Poetry Posse 2015
Jamie Bond * Gail Weston Shazor * Albert 'Infinite' Carrasco
Siddartha Beth Pierce * Janet P. Caldwell * Tony Henninger
Joe DaVerbal Minddancer * Neetu Wali * Shareef Abdur – Rasheed
Kimberly Burnham * Ann White * Keith Alan Hamilton
Katherine Wyatt * Fahredin Shehu * Hülya N. Yılmaz
Teresa E. Gallion * Jackie Allen * William S. Peters, Sr.

Now Available

www.innerchildpress.com/the-year-of-the-poet

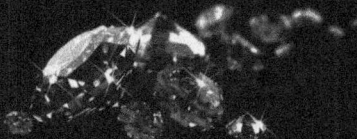

The Year of the Poet II
September 2015

Featured Poets

Alfreda Ghee * Lonneice Weeks Badley * Demetrios Trifiatis

Sapphires

The Poetry Posse 2015

Jamie Bond * Gail Weston Shazor * Albert 'Infinite' Carrasco
Siddartha Beth Pierce * Janet P. Caldwell * Tony Henninger
Joe DaVerbal Minddancer * Neetu Wali * Shareef Abdur – Rasheed
Kimberly Burnham * Ann White * Keith Alan Hamilton
Katherine Wyatt * Fahredin Shehu * Hülya N. Yılmaz
Teresa E. Gallion * Jackie Allen * William S. Peters, Sr.

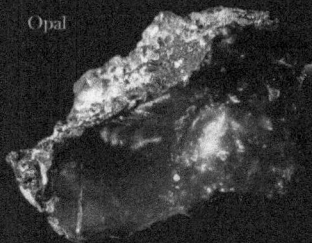

The Year of the Poet II
October 2015

Featured Poets

Monte Smith * Laura J. Wolfe * William Washington

Opal

The Poetry Posse 2015

Jamie Bond * Gail Weston Shazor * Albert 'Infinite' Carrasco
Siddartha Beth Pierce * Janet P. Caldwell * Tony Henninger
Joe DaVerbal Minddancer * Neetu Wali * Shareef Abdur – Rasheed
Kimberly Burnham * Ann White * Keith Alan Hamilton
Katherine Wyatt * Fahredin Shehu * Hülya N. Yılmaz
Teresa E. Gallion * Jackie Allen * William S. Peters, Sr.

The Year of the Poet II
November 2015

Featured Poets

Alan W. Jankowski
Bijnay Mohanty
James Moore

Topaz

The Poetry Posse 2015

Jamie Bond * Gail Weston Shazor * Albert 'Infinite' Carrasco
Siddartha Beth Pierce * Janet P. Caldwell * Tony Henninger
Joe DaVerbal Minddancer * Neetu Wali * Shareef Abdur – Rasheed
Kimberly Burnham * Ann White * Keith Alan Hamilton
Katherine Wyatt * Fahredin Shehu * Hülya N. Yılmaz
Teresa E. Gallion * Jackie Allen * William S. Peters, Sr.

The Year of the Poet II
December 2015

Featured Poets

Kerione Bryan * Michelle Joan Barulich * Neville Hiatt

Turquoise

The Poetry Posse 2015

Jamie Bond * Gail Weston Shazor * Albert 'Infinite' Carrasco
Siddartha Beth Pierce * Janet P. Caldwell * Tony Henninger
Joe DaVerbal Minddancer * Neetu Wali * Shareef Abdur – Rasheed
Kimberly Burnham * Ann White * Keith Alan Hamilton
Katherine Wyatt * Fahredin Shehu * Hülya N. Yılmaz
Teresa E. Gallion * Jackie Allen * William S. Peters, Sr.

Now Available

www.innerchildpress.com/the-year-of-the-poet

The Year of the Poet III
January 2016

Featured Poets
Lana Joseph * Atom Cyrus Rush * Christena Williams

Dark-eyed Junco

The Poetry Posse 2016
Gail Weston Shazor * Anne Jakuboczk Vel Batyryldaun * Alan J. White
Fahredin Shehu * Hrishikesh Padhye * Janet P. Caldwell
Joe DaVerbal Minddancer * Shareef Abdur ~ Rasheed
Albert Carrasco * Kimberly Burnham * Keith Alan Hamilton
Hülya N. Yılmaz * Demetrios Trifiatis * Alan W. Jankowski
Teresa E. Gallion * Jackie Davis Allen * William S. Peters, Sr.

The Year of the Poet III
February 2016

Featured Poets
Anthony Arnold
Anna Chalasz
Andre Fau shema

Puffin

The Poetry Posse 2016
Gail Weston Shazor * Joe DaVerbal Minddancer * Alfreda Ghee
Fahredin Shehu * Hrishikesh Padhye * Janet P. Caldwell
Anne Jakuboczk Vel Batyryldaun * Shareef Abdur ~ Rasheed
Albert Carrasco * Kimberly Burnham * Alan J. White
Hülya N. Yılmaz * Demetrios Trifiatis * Alan W. Jankowski
Teresa E. Gallion * Jackie Davis Allen * William S. Peters, Sr.

The Year of the Poet
March 2016

Featured Poets
Jeton Kelmendi   Nizar Sartawi   Sami Muhanna

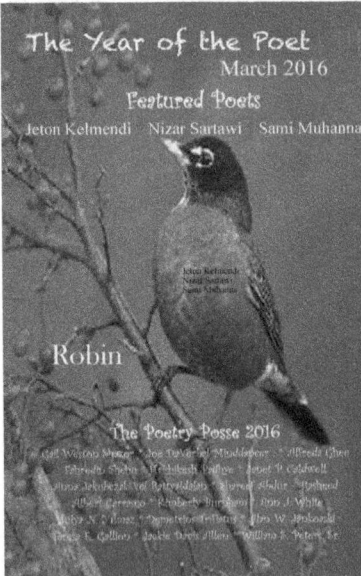

Robin

The Poetry Posse 2016
Gail Weston Shazor * Joe DaVerbal Minddancer * Alfreda Ghee
Fahredin Shehu * Hrishikesh Padhye * Janet P. Caldwell
Anne Jakuboczk Vel Batyryldaun * Shareef Abdur ~ Rasheed
Albert Carrasco * Kimberly Burnham * Alan J. White
Hülya N. Yılmaz * Demetrios Trifiatis * Alan W. Jankowski
Teresa E. Gallion * Jackie Davis Allen * William S. Peters, Sr.

The Year of the Poet III

Featured Poets
Ali Abdolrezaei
Anna Chalasz
Agim Vinca
Ceri Naz

Black Capped Chickadee

The Poetry Posse 2016
Gail Weston Shazor * Joe DaVerbal Minddancer * Alfreda Ghee
Fahredin Shehu * Hrishikesh Padhye * Janet P. Caldwell
Anne Jakuboczk Vel Batyryldaun * Shareef Abdur ~ Rasheed
Albert Carrasco * Kimberly Burnham * Alan J. White
Hülya N. Yılmaz * Demetrios Trifiatis * Alan W. Jankowski
Teresa E. Gallion * Jackie Davis Allen * William S. Peters, Sr.

celebrating international poetry month

Now Available

www.innerchildpress.com/the-year-of-the-poet

The Year of the Poet
May 2016

Bob Strum
Barbara Allan
D.L. Davis

Oriole

The Year of the Poet III
June 2016

Featured Poets

Qibrije Demiri- Frangu
Naime Beqiraj
Faleeha Hassan
Bedri Zyberaj

Black Necked Stilt

The Poetry Posse 2016

Featured Poets

Tram Fatima 'Ashi'
Langley Shazor
Jody Doty
Emilia T. Davis

Indigo Bunting

The Poetry Posse 2016

The Year of the Poet III
August 2016

Featured Poets

Anita Dash
Irena Jovanovic
Malgorzata Gouluda

Painted Bunting

The Poetry Posse 2016

Now Available

www.innerchildpress.com/the-year-of-the-poet

Inner Child Press Anthologies

Now Available

www.innerchildpress.com/the-year-of-the-poet

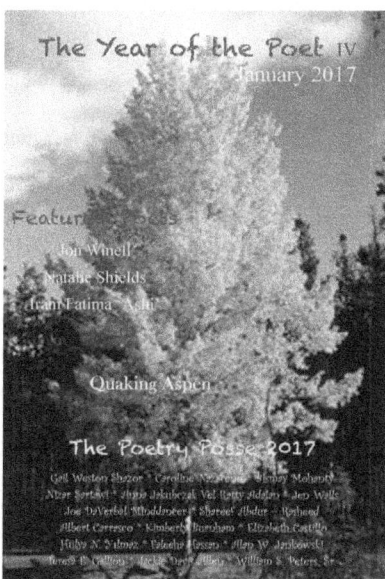

The Year of the Poet IV
January 2017

Featured Poets
Jon Winell
Natalie Shields
Jeani Fatima 'Ashi

Quaking Aspen

The Poetry Posse 2017

Gail Weston Shazor * Caroline Nazareno * Tzemay Mohanty
Nizar Sartawi * Shina Jakubczak Vel Ratty Adalan * Jen Walls
Joe DaVerbal Minddancer * Shareef Abdur – Rasheed
Albert Carrasco * Kimberly Burnham * Elizabeth Castillo
Hülya N. Yılmaz * Fahreha Hassan * Alan W. Jankowski
Teresa E. Gallion * Jackie Davis Allen * William S. Peters, Sr.

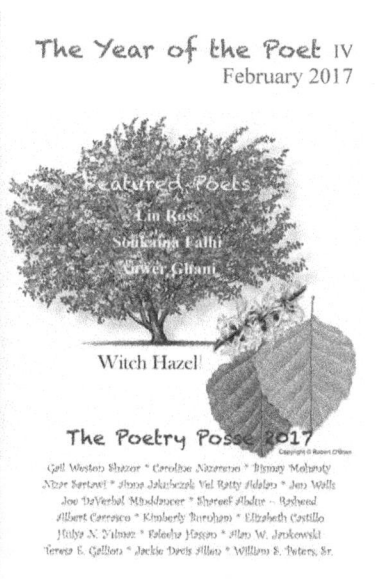

The Year of the Poet IV
February 2017

Featured Poets
Lin Ross
Soukaina Fathi
Anwer Ghani

Witch Hazel

The Poetry Posse 2017

Gail Weston Shazor * Caroline Nazareno * Tzemay Mohanty
Nizar Sartawi * Shina Jakubczak Vel Ratty Adalan * Jen Walls
Joe DaVerbal Minddancer * Shareef Abdur – Rasheed
Albert Carrasco * Kimberly Burnham * Elizabeth Castillo
Hülya N. Yılmaz * Fahreha Hassan * Alan W. Jankowski
Teresa E. Gallion * Jackie Davis Allen * William S. Peters, Sr.

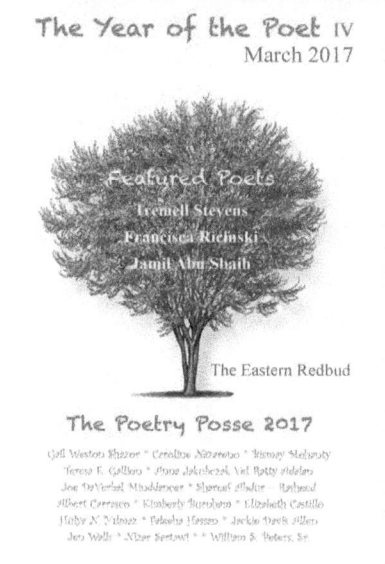

The Year of the Poet IV
March 2017

Featured Poets
Tremell Stevens
Francisca Ricinski
Jamil Abu Shaih

The Eastern Redbud

The Poetry Posse 2017

Gail Weston Shazor * Caroline Nazareno * Tzemay Mohanty
Teresa E. Gallion * Shina Jakubczak Vel Ratty Adalan
Joe DaVerbal Minddancer * Shareef Abdur – Rasheed
Albert Carrasco * Kimberly Burnham * Elizabeth Castillo
Hülya N. Yılmaz * Fahreha Hassan * Jackie Davis Allen
Jen Walls * Nizar Sartawi * * William S. Peters, Sr.

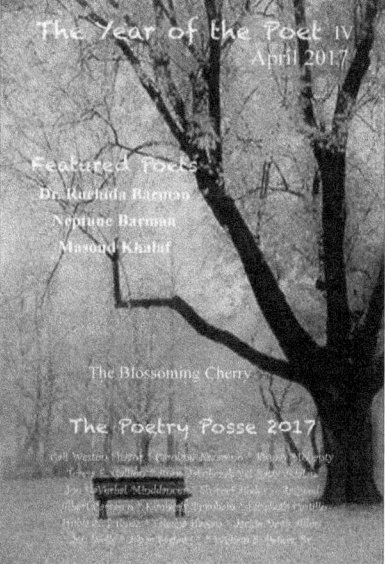

The Year of the Poet IV
April 2017

Featured Poets
Dr. Ruchida Barman
Neptune Barman
Masood Khalaf

The Blossoming Cherry

The Poetry Posse 2017

Gail Weston Shazor * Caroline Nazareno * Tzemay Mohanty
Teresa E. Gallion * Shina Jakubczak Vel Ratty Adalan
Joe DaVerbal Minddancer * Shareef Abdur – Rasheed
Albert Carrasco * Kimberly Burnham * Elizabeth Castillo
Hülya N. Yılmaz * Fahreha Hassan * Jackie Davis Allen
Jen Walls * Nizar Sartawi * * William S. Peters, Sr.

Now Available

www.innerchildpress.com/the-year-of-the-poet

The Year of the Poet IV
May 2017

The Flowering Dogwood Tree

Featured Poets
Kallisa Powell
Alicja Maria Kuberska
Fethi Sassi

The Poetry Posse 2017

Gail Weston Shazor * Caroline Nazareno * Hussey Mohouty
Teresa E. Gallion * Anne Jakubczak Vel Ratty Adalan
Joe DaVerbal Minddancer * Shareef Abdur - Rasheed
Albert Carrasco * Kimberly Burnham * Elizabeth Castillo
Hülya N. Yılmaz * Paula Hyssen * Jackie Davis Allen
Jen Walls * Nizar Sartawi * * William S. Peters, Sr.

The Year of the Poet IV
June 2017

Featured Poets
Eliza Segiet
Tze-Min Tsai
Abdulla Issa

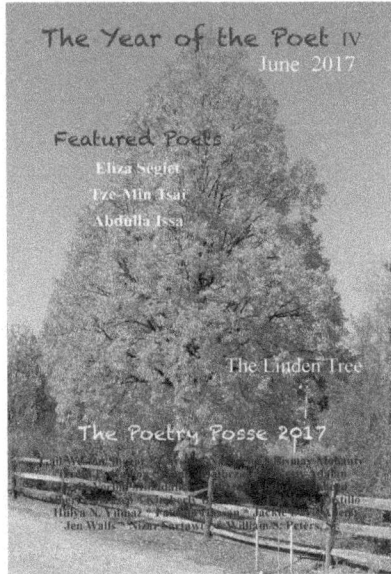

The Linden Tree

The Poetry Posse 2017

Hülya N. Yılmaz * Paula Hyssen * Jackie Davis Allen
Jen Walls * Nizar Sartawi * * William S. Peters, Sr.

The Year of the Poet IV
July 2017

Featured Poets
Anca Mihaela Bruma
Ibaa Ismail
Zvonko Taneski

The Oak Moon

The Poetry Posse 2017

Gail Weston Shazor * Caroline Nazareno * Hussey Mohouty
Teresa E. Gallion * Anne Jakubczak Vel Ratty Adalan
Joe DaVerbal Minddancer * Shareef Abdur - Rasheed
Albert Carrasco * Kimberly Burnham * Elizabeth Castillo
Hülya N. Yılmaz * Paula Hyssen * Jackie Davis Allen
Jen Walls * Nizar Sartawi * * William S. Peters, Sr.

The Year of the Poet IV
August 2017

Featured Poets
Jonathan Aquino
Kitty Hsu
Langley Shazor

The Hazelnut Tree

The Poetry Posse 2017

Gail Weston Shazor * Caroline Nazareno *
Teresa E. Gallion * Anne Jakubczak Vel Ratty Adalan
Joe DaVerbal Minddancer * Shareef Abdur - Rasheed
Albert Carrasco * Kimberly Burnham * Elizabeth Castillo
Hülya N. Yılmaz * Paula Hyssen * Jackie Davis Allen
Jen Walls * Nizar Sartawi * * William S. Peters, Sr.

Now Available

www.innerchildpress.com/the-year-of-the-poet

The Year of the Poet IV
September 2017

Featured Poets

Martina Reisz Newberry
Ameer Nassir
Christine Fulco Neal
Robert Neal

The Elm Tree

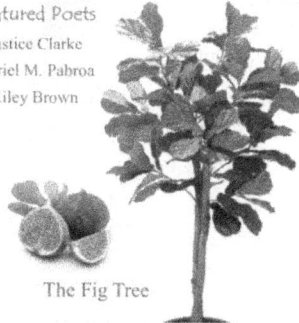

The Poetry Posse 2017

Gail Weston Shazor * Caroline Nazareno * Bismay Mohanty
Teresa E. Gallion * Anna Jakubczak Vel Ratty Adalan
Joe DaVerbal Minddancer * Shareef Abdur – Rasheed
Albert Carrasco * Kimberly Burnham * Elizabeth Castillo
Hülya N. Yılmaz * Faleeha Hassan * Jackie Davis Allen
Jen Walls * Nizar Sartawi * * William S. Peters, Sr.

The Year of the Poet IV
October 2017

Featured Poets

Ahmed Abu Saleem
Nedal Al-Qaeim
Sadeddin Shahin

The Black Walnut Tree

The Poetry Posse 2017

Gail Weston Shazor * Caroline Nazareno * Bismay Mohanty
Teresa E. Gallion * Anna Jakubczak Vel Ratty Adalan
Joe DaVerbal Minddancer * Shareef Abdur – Rasheed
Albert Carrasco * Kimberly Burnham * Elizabeth Castillo
Hülya N. Yılmaz * Faleeha Hassan * Jackie Davis Allen
Jen Walls * Nizar Sartawi * * William S. Peters, Sr.

The Year of the Poet IV
November 2017

Featured Poets

Kay Peters
Alfreda D. Ghee
Gabriella Garofalo
Rosemary Cappello

The Tree of Life

The Poetry Posse 2017

Gail Weston Shazor * Caroline Nazareno * Bismay Mohanty
Teresa E. Gallion * Anna Jakubczak Vel Ratty Adalan
Joe DaVerbal Minddancer * Shareef Abdur – Rasheed
Albert Carrasco * Kimberly Burnham * Elizabeth Castillo
Hülya N. Yılmaz * Faleeha Hassan * Jackie Davis Allen
Jen Walls * Nizar Sartawi * William S. Peters, Sr.

The Year of the Poet IV
December 2017

Featured Poets

Justice Clarke
Mariel M. Pabroa
Kiley Brown

The Fig Tree

The Poetry Posse 2017

Gail Weston Shazor * Caroline Nazareno * Bismay Mohanty
Teresa E. Gallion * Anna Jakubczak Vel Ratty Adalan
Joe DaVerbal Minddancer * Shareef Abdur – Rasheed
Albert Carrasco * Kimberly Burnham * Elizabeth Castillo
Hülya N. Yılmaz * Faleeha Hassan * Jackie Davis Allen
Jen Walls * Nizar Sartawi * William S. Peters, Sr.

Now Available

www.innerchildpress.com/the-year-of-the-poet

The Year of the Poet V
January 2018

Featured Poets

Iyad Shamasnah

Yasmeen Hamzeh

Ali Abdolrezaei

Aksum

The Poetry Posse 2018

Gail Weston Shazor * Caroline Nazareno * Tezmin Ition Tsai
Hülya N. Yılmaz * Faleeha Hassan * Jackie Davis Allen
Teresa E. Gallion * Anna Jakubczak Vel Ratty Adalan
Alicja Maria Kuberska * Shareef Abdur – Rasheed
Kimberly Burnham * Elizabeth Castillo
Nizar Sartawi * William S. Peters, Sr.

The Year of the Poet V
February 2018

Sabean

Featured Poets

Muhammad Azrani

Anna Szawracka

Abhilipsa Kuanar

Aanika Aery

The Poetry Posse 2018

Gail Weston Shazor * Caroline Nazareno * Tezmin Ition Tsai
Hülya N. Yılmaz * Faleeha Hassan * Jackie Davis Allen
Teresa E. Gallion * Anna Jakubczak Vel Ratty Adalan
Alicja Maria Kuberska * Shareef Abdur – Rasheed
Kimberly Burnham * Elizabeth Castillo
Nizar Sartawi * William S. Peters, Sr.

The Year of the Poet V
March 2018

Featured Poets

Iram Fatima 'Ashi'
Cassandra Swan
Jaleel Khazaal
Shazia Zaman

Mexico   Cuba

Caribbean
&
Middle America

The Poetry Posse 2018

Gail Weston Shazor * Nizar Sartawi * Hülya N. Yılmaz
Jackie Davis Allen * Caroline 'Ceri' Nazareno
Alicja Maria Kuberska * Teresa E. Gallion
Faleeha Hassan * Shareef Abdur – Rasheed
Kimberly Burnham * Elizabeth Castillo
Tezmin Ition Tsai * William S. Peters, Sr.

The Year of the Poet V
April 2018

Featured Poets

The Nez Perce

The Poetry Posse 2018

Now Available

www.innerchildpress.com/the-year-of-the-poet

The Year of the Poet V
May 2018

Featured Poets
Zaldy Carreon de Leon Jr.
Sylwia K. Malinowska
Lindita Ahmeti
Otelia Prodan

The Sumerians

The Poetry Posse 2018

Gail Weston Shazor * Nizar Sartawi * Hülya N. Yılmaz
Jackie Davis Allen * Caroline 'Ceri' Nazareno
Alicja Maria Kuberska * Teresa E. Gallion
Kimberly Burnham * Shareef Abdur – Rasheed
Faleeha Hassan * Elizabeth Castillo * Swapna Behera
Tezmin Ition Tsai * William S. Peters, Sr.

The Year of the Poet V
June 2018

Featured Poets
Bilall Maliqi * Daim Miftari * Gojko Božović * Sofija Živković

The Paleo Indians

The Poetry Posse 2018

Gail Weston Shazor * Nizar Sartawi * Hülya N. Yılmaz
Jackie Davis Allen * Caroline 'Ceri' Nazareno
Alicja Maria Kuberska * Teresa E. Gallion
Kimberly Burnham * Shareef Abdur – Rasheed
Faleeha Hassan * Elizabeth Castillo * Swapna Behera
Tezmin Ition Tsai * William S. Peters, Sr.

The Year of the Poet V
July 2018

Featured Poets
Padmaja Iyengar-Paddy
Mohammad Ikbal Hank
Eliza Segiet
Tom Higgins

Oceania

The Poetry Posse 2018

Gail Weston Shazor * Nizar Sartawi * Hülya N. Yılmaz
Jackie Davis Allen * Caroline 'Ceri' Nazareno
Alicja Maria Kuberska * Teresa E. Gallion
Kimberly Burnham * Shareef Abdur – Rasheed
Faleeha Hassan * Elizabeth Castillo * Swapna Behera
Tezmin Ition Tsai * William S. Peters, Sr.

The Year of the Poet V
August 2018

Featured Poets
Hussein Habasch * Mircea Dan Duta * Naida Mujkič * Swagat Das

The Lapita

The Poetry Posse 2018

Gail Weston Shazor * Nizar Sartawi * Hülya N. Yılmaz
Jackie Davis Allen * Caroline 'Ceri' Nazareno
Alicja Maria Kuberska * Teresa E. Gallion
Kimberly Burnham * Shareef Abdur – Rasheed
Ashok K. Bhargava* Elizabeth Castillo * Swapna Behaera
Tezmin Ition Tsai * William S. Peters, Sr.

Now Available

www.innerchildpress.com/the-year-of-the-poet

194

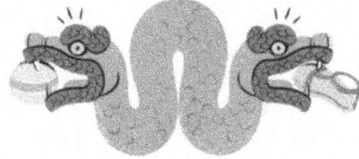

and there is much, much more !

visit . . .

www.innerchildpress.com/antho
logies-sales-special.php

Also check out our Authors and
all the wonderful Books
Available at :

www.innerchildpress.com/autho
rs-pages

INNER CHILD PRESS

WORLD HEALING WORLD PEACE

2018

A Poetry Anthology for Humanity

Now Available

www.worldhealingworldpeacepoetry.com

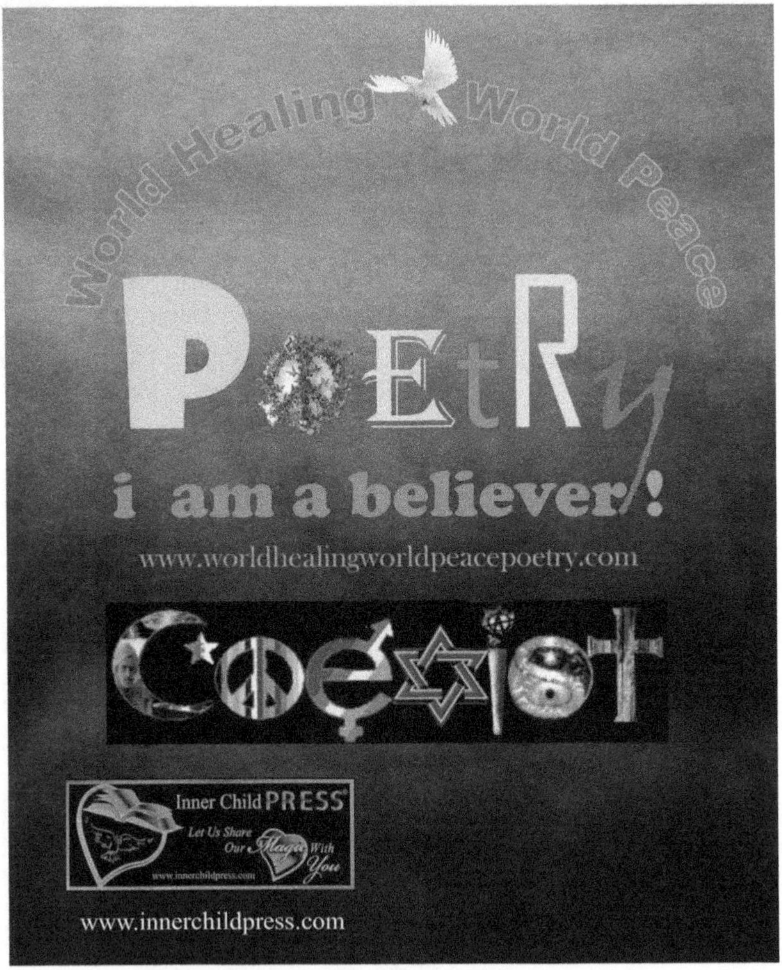

Now Available

www.worldhealingworldpeacepoetry.com

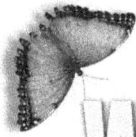

I support

World Healing World Peace

www.worldhealingworldpeacepoetry.com

World Healing
World Peace
2018

Now Available

www.worldhealingworldpeacepoetry.com

Inner Child Press International

'building bridges of cultural understanding'

Meet the Board of Directors

www.innerchildpress.com

Inner Child Press International

'building bridges of cultural understanding'

Meet our Cultural Ambassadors

Fahredin Shehu
Director of Cultural

Faleha Hassan
Iraq – USA

Elizabeth E. Castillo
Philippines

Antoinette Coleman
Chicago
Midwest USA

Ananda Nepali
Nepal – Tibet
Northern India

Kimberly Burnham
Pacific Southwest
USA

Alicja Kuberska
Poland
Eastern Europe

Swapna Behera
India
Southeast Asia

Kolade O. Freedom
Nigeria
West Africa

Mousif Beroual
Morocco
Northern Africa

Ashok K. Bhargava
Canada

Tzemin Ition Tsai
Republic of China
Greater China

Alicia M. Ramírez
Mexico
Central America

Christena AV Williams
Jamaica
Caribbean

Louise Hudon
Eastern Canada

Aziz Mountassir
Morocco
Northern Africa

Shareef Abdur-Rasheed
Southeastern USA

Laure Charazac
France
Western Europe

Mohammad Ikbal Harb
Lebanon
Middle East

Mohammed Abdel
Aziz Shmeis
Egypt
Middle East

Bhary Mainga
Kenya
Eastern Africa

Josephus R. Johnson
Liberia

www.innerchildpress.com

202

This Anthological Publication
is underwritten solely by

Inner Child Press

Inner Child Press is a Publishing Company Founded and Operated by Writers. Our personal publishing experiences provides us an intimate understanding of the sometimes daunting challenges Writers, New and Seasoned may face in the Business of Publishing and Marketing their Creative "Written Work".

For more Information

Inner Child Press

www.innerchildpress.com

Inner Child Press International

'building bridges of cultural understanding'

202 Wiltree Court, State College, Pennsylvania 16801

www.innerchildpress.com

~ *fini* ~